THE
BEATLES
IN 100 OBJECTS

STERLING
New York

An Imprint of Sterling Publishing
387 Park Avenue South
New York, NY 10016

© 2013 by Carlton Books Ltd
For photographic copyright information, please see picture credits on page 256

ISBN 978-1-4549-0986-6

For information about custom editions, special sales, and premium and corporate purchases, please contact Sterling Special Sales at 800-805-5489 or specialsales@sterlingpublishing.com.

Printed and bound in Dubai

2 4 6 8 10 9 7 5 3 1

www.sterlingpublishing.com

THE
BEATLES
IN 100 OBJECTS

THE STORY OF THE WORLD'S GREATEST ROCK-AND-ROLL BAND
THROUGH THE ITEMS THEY USED, CREATED, AND INSPIRED

BRIAN SOUTHALL

STERLING
New York

Contents

Introduction

by Brian Southall

Being involved with this book turned out to be more than just a basic double whammy. In addition to assisting in the discovery and compiling of the various objects – and also doing some writing – the whole enjoyable exercise ultimately turned out to be an almanac of my own youth.

Bringing together this wide-ranging collection of 100 fascinating and significant objects from the lifetime of the Beatles brought back memories of 1962 when, as a 15-year-old schoolboy, I heard 'Love Me Do' for the first time. I was hooked and stuck with the Beatles through the swingin' sixties and beyond.

As they grew in popularity to top the charts and fill concert halls, their story unfolded to encompass nationwide success and ultimately global domination on a scale never seen before by any pop artist. And they took me and a host of like-minded adolescents along with them on the journey of a lifetime. We bought their records, tuned in to their radio shows, watched their TV appearances and, if you were lucky, actually got hold of a ticket to see (if not hear) them in the flesh.

Under the watchful eye of manager Brian Epstein, the 'fab four' – John Lennon, Paul McCartney, George Harrison and eventually Ringo Starr – grew from a mop-top pop group into a unique musical entity which changed both the look and sound of popular music.

Fifty years on from the release of their first album and the arrival of Beatlemania, we're looking back and celebrating their progress as they upgraded their instruments, changed their appearance, travelled the world to satisfy their army of fans, continually introduced new musical styles and eventually fell out and broke up. As pop idols, the Beatles influenced music and fashion but they also had a profound effect on people's attitudes towards sex, drugs, religion and politics. And all this was played out in front of a gigantic worldwide audience which clung limpet-like to every note, every word, every news item, every photograph and every bit of gossip.

This collection of memorable and influential objects – including instruments, records, contracts, tickets, memorabilia and a host of personal items – celebrates the most momentous achievements and landmark moments in the life of the Beatles. For those who weren't around at the time, the Beatles launched *Mersey Beat*, led the British pop invasion of America, created the concept album and embraced psychedelia before ending their career as the world's biggest selling pop act of all time.

So, while I was just one of the millions of fans whose life was influenced by the Beatles, it turned out that I was also one of the lucky ones because my life continued to be affected by them even after they had broken up. Working at EMI – long the home to the Beatles and their music – in the 1970s meant that I was involved in various solo recordings by the ex-Beatles and as a result met and spent time with each of them except John, of course, who sent his instructions and comments via phone calls, telegrams and postcards.

So here we have a book which doesn't just bring together for the first time a unique collection of objects which illustrate and highlight the life and times of the Beatles in a new and informative way but also reminds at least one senior citizen – and everybody else who is remotely interested in the most golden years of pop music – of how it was back then ... when Beatles Ruled The World.

Brian Southall, Great Baddow, Essex

The Beatles' first ever television appearance: Granada TV's *People And Places* on October 17, 1962.

Antoria guitar

Paul's borrowed instrument for the Quarrymen

When Paul McCartney first played his guitar to John Lennon and the rest of the assembled Quarrymen in July 1957, it seems that he was forced to borrow a guitar from one of the other band members, turn it upside down (as he was left-handed) and play well enough to get Lennon and his mates to invite him to join their group.

As a fully-fledged band member, McCartney decided it would be better if he had a guitar of his own, so he took the trumpet his father had given him and traded it in for a six-string Zenith Model 17 guitar worth about £14. This was the guitar he used throughout the majority of the Quarrymen's gigs between 1957 and 1960 when, soon after his 18th birthday, he bought a £20 Rosetti Solid 7 guitar on hire purchase from Hessy's music store in Liverpool.

Even though he had owned a guitar since 1957, it seems that McCartney didn't always carry it with him. On occasions when he and his friends played together for fun, he was forced to borrow one – and the Antoria acoustic guitar was one he borrowed from local lad Dennis Littler who often joined McCartney, Lennon and George Harrison during their early 'jam' sessions, which often took place at the home of McCartney's Auntie Jin.

Auntie Jin (or Gin) was the youngest sister of McCartney's father James and following the death of McCartney's mother, she and he sister opened their homes up to McCartney and his brother Mike. In fact it was in her Huyton home that McCartney held his 21st birthday party in 1963.

According to Littler, who was also in a local Liverpool band, he paid £19 on hire purchase for his Antoria guitar which seemingly has the unique distinction of being borrowed and played by each of the future Beatles. The Antoria guitar had been in introduced into Britain in the late 1950s by the J T Coppock company of Leeds who imported them from Japan and both Hank Marvin of the Shadows and singer Marty Wilde used Antorias while drummer Ringo Starr was once pictured playing a model during his time with Rory Storm and the Hurricanes.

After Coppock ceased trading in the 1980s, the Antoria brand name was picked up by another British company who assigned it to guitars that were made in South Korea, and Oasis leader Noel Gallagher was filmed using an Antoria J200 model in the video for the single 'Wonderwall'.

The natural wood-coloured Antoria owned by Littler and borrowed by McCartney in the late fifties was sold at auction in London in 2012 for over £43,000 when it appeared with a letter signed by McCartney that confirmed, "I well remember the parties at my Auntie Jin's house where we would often bring our guitars and play. Dennis would often join in and on the occasions when we forgot to bring our own guitars Dennis would kindly lend us his to play on."

(Right) The Antoria guitar that Paul McCartney borrowed from a friend and played at parties at his auntie's house.

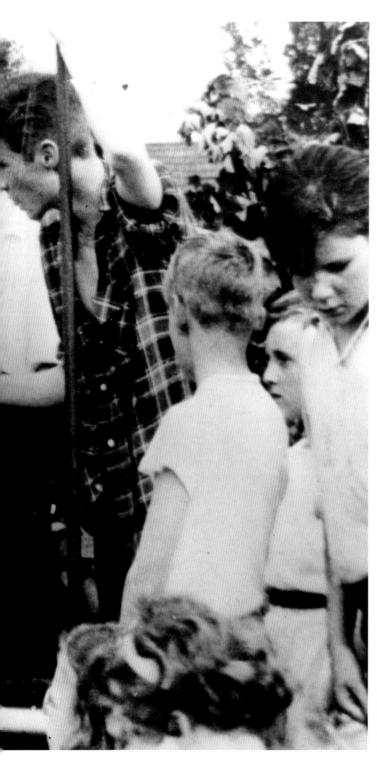

John Lennon at the microphone,
leading the Quarrymen at the garden fete in
Woolton, July 1957. It was here that Lennon
first met Paul McCartney, who was in the
crowd that day at St Peter's Parish Church.

Programme from the Liverpool Empire

Getting started

In his quest for success as a musician, John Lennon's first step on the road to fame and fortune came way back in June 1957 when his group the Quarrymen took part in a talent show at Liverpool's historic Empire Theatre.

The group began with Lennon and his school friend Pete Shotton and also involved Rod Davis, Eric Griffiths, Colin Hanton, Len Garry, Ivan Vaughan and Nigel Whalley, although the exact line-up for their local qualifying heat of famous TV talent scout Carroll Levis' *TV Star Search* on the afternoon of Sunday June 9 is unclear. What is clear is that the Quarrymen, named after the Quarry Bank school attended by Lennon and Shotton, failed at the first attempt and were rejected from this preliminary audition which lasted just three minutes and involved the group playing 'Worried Man Blues'.

They lost out to the Sunnyside Skiffle Group – who boasted a midget lead singer – but undaunted Lennon took his second group, by now consisting of Paul McCartney and George Harrison and called Johnny and the Moondogs back to the Empire in October 1958 for another crack at *TV Star Search*. This time they won through to the local final of Levis' talent show – also held in October – and from there went to qualify for a further final held at Manchester's Hippodrome Theatre on November 15, 1958 but, short of money, the three band members had to get a train back to Liverpool before the final judging took place.

The Liverpool Empire was opened in 1925 in Lime Street and could hold a packed house of over 2,300 people. It featured performances by most of the major acts in British music hall and post World War II entertainment and McCartney once boasted that he had an 'in' at the theatre – "one of my relatives was a stage door keeper and he'd get autographs for me", he said while he also collected them himself at the stage door.

Before he went on stage with the Moondogs, Harrison had also visited the Empire to see the music stars of the day. "I went to the Liverpool Empire in 1956 to see Lonnie Donegan and people like Danny and the Juniors and the Crew Cuts."

The Beatles first appearance at the Empire came in October 1962 on a show presented by manager Brian Epstein's newly formed NEMS Enterprises and local club owner Ray McFall when they joined Little Richard, Craig Douglas, Kenny Lynch, Jet Harris and Sounds Incorporated as part of a 'pop package' with shows at 5.40pm and 8.00pm during which they played four numbers and backed Douglas during his set.

They returned to the Empire four times in 1963 – firstly in March during their UK tour with Tommy Roe and Chris Montez and then again in May with Roy Orbison and twice more at the end of the year when a special edition of the TV show Juke Boxy Jury was filmed in the theatre on December 7 followed by a preview performance of *The Beatles Christmas Show* three days before Christmas.

They returned the following year – on November 8 – as part of their UK tour and on December 5, 1964 played their last ever live concert in Liverpool at the Empire Theatre when over 40,000 fans applied for tickets to see them at the place where they had failed their first audition eight years earlier.

(Right) A ticket and programme for the Beatles' debut show at the Liverpool Empire in October 1962, where they were third on the bill.

EMPIRE
LIVERPOOL

LITTLE RICHARD

2nd Performance. 8-0

SUNDAY
OCTOBER **28**

ORCH. STALLS
12 /6

F22

TO BE RETAINED

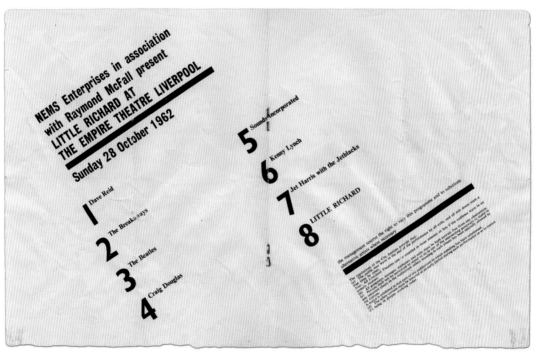

NEMS Enterprises in association
with Raymond McFall present
LITTLE RICHARD AT
THE EMPIRE THEATRE LIVERPOOL

Sunday 28 October 1962

1 Dave Reid

2 The Breakaways

3 The Beatles

4 Craig Douglas

5 Sounds Incorporated

6 Kenny Lynch

7 Jet Harris with the Jetblacks

8 LITTLE RICHARD

the management reserve the right so vary this programme and to substitute
alternative artists where necessary

Poster from the Cavern Club

The local

By the time the Beatles played their first show in Liverpool's most popular cellar club, the Cavern had been open for four years and was well established as a venue for jazz and skiffle bands. Located in Matthew Street, it officially opened on January 16, 1957, with local jazz band the Merseysippi topping the bill.

The original owner was Alan Sytner, who put on jazz shows at the Temple restaurant and during a trip to Paris had visited *Le Caveau Francais* Jazz Club and was inspired to open the Cavern in an old wine and spirits store room. On August 7, 1957, an up-and-coming skiffle band called the Quarrymen were booked to play at the Cavern and that was when John Lennon first stood on the stage at the Cavern – but on this occasion without Paul McCartney, who was away at scout camp.

In fact, Lennon's attempt that night to add rock 'n' roll to the show with a version of Elvis Presley's 'Hound Dog' and 'Blue Suede Shoes' brought a terse response from Quarrymen Rod Davis and club owner Sytner who sent the singer a note saying 'cut out the bloody rock!' For the next three years – during which time Ray McFall bought the club in October 1959 for £2,750 – the Cavern remained true to its jazz and skiffle heritage, but as rock and pop began to grow in popularity so the Cavern embraced the new music and in May 1960 a rock 'n' roll evening was held in the club with Cass & the Casanovas and Rory Storm & the Hurricanes (who featured a drummer named Ringo Starr) on the bill.

The Beatles – Lennon, McCartney, Harrison and Pete Best – made their debut at the Cavern on February 21, 1961, when they played a lunchtime show which was followed by two evening performances in other local venues on the same day. A month later on March 21, the group made their evening debut at the Cavern and McCartney remembers the club as "sweaty, damp, dark, loud and exciting" while Lennon recalled, "In those old Cavern days half the thing was just ad lib, what you'd

call comedy. We just used to mess about, jump into the audience, do anything."

On November 9, 1961 local record shop owner Brian Epstein visited the club to watch the Beatles' lunchtime show. His arrival prompted resident disc jockey Bob Wooler to tell the audience, "We have with us a Mr Epstein, who owns NEMS" while Harrison explained, "He stood at the back listening and afterwards came round to the band room. We thought he was some very posh rich fellow. He had wanted us to sign up but I believe he came a few times before he actually decided to be our manager."

By the autumn of 1963, the Beatles had made a total of 274 appearances at the Cavern in a two-and-a-half year period. Their last ever show in the place where their careers were probably launched was on August 3, 1963.

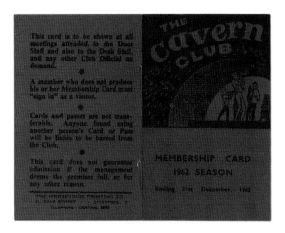

(Above) A Cavern Club membership card for the 1962 'season'.

(Right) A Cavern hand bill from 1963 advertising three shows and a Good Friday 'R&B Marathon', featuring the Beatles and eight other groups.

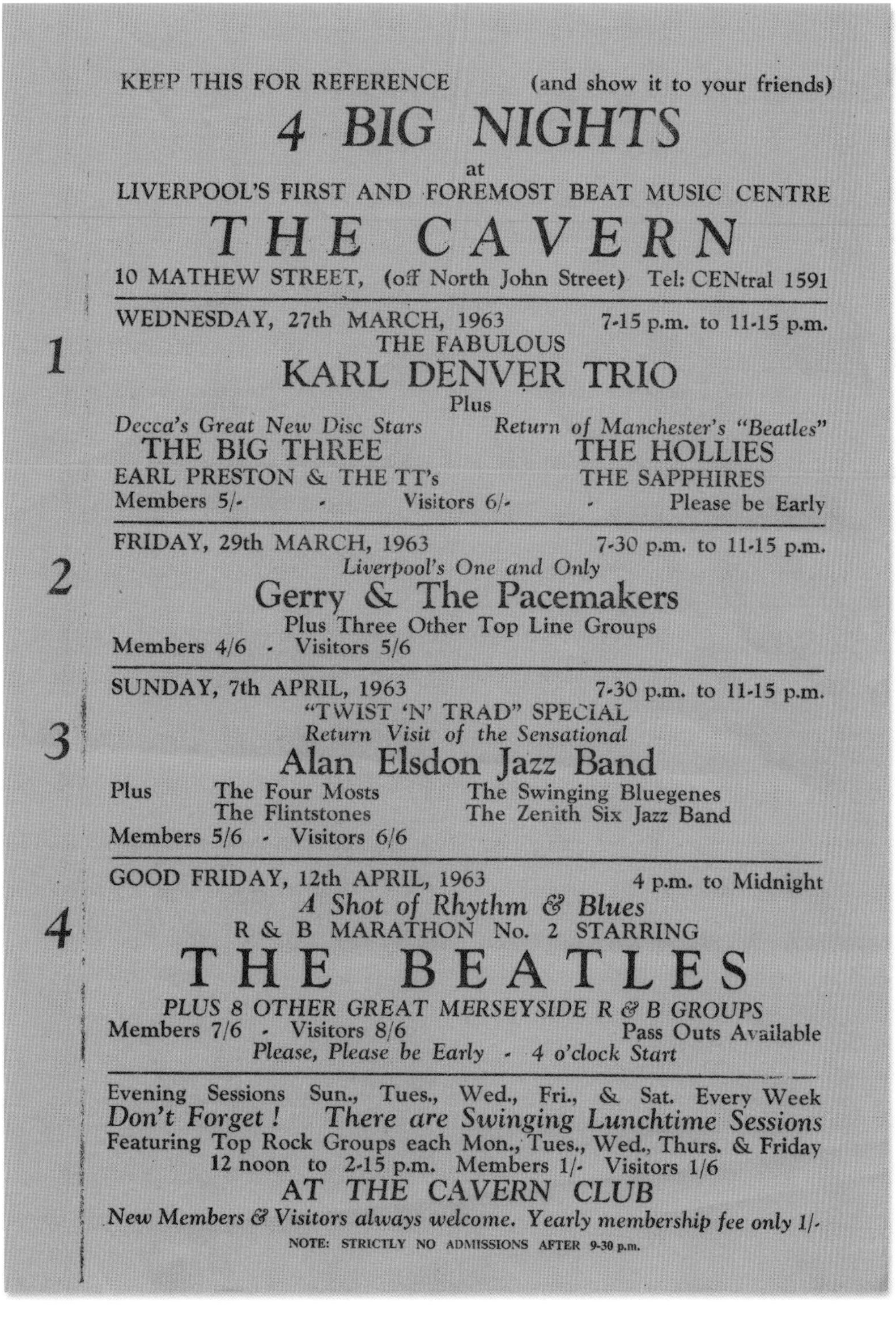

KEEP THIS FOR REFERENCE   (and show it to your friends)

4 BIG NIGHTS

at

LIVERPOOL'S FIRST AND FOREMOST BEAT MUSIC CENTRE

THE CAVERN

10 MATHEW STREET, (off North John Street) Tel: CENtral 1591

1

WEDNESDAY, 27th MARCH, 1963   7-15 p.m. to 11-15 p.m.

THE FABULOUS

KARL DENVER TRIO

Plus

Decca's Great New Disc Stars   Return of Manchester's "Beatles"

THE BIG THREE   THE HOLLIES

EARL PRESTON & THE TT's   THE SAPPHIRES

Members 5/-   ·   Visitors 6/-   ·   Please be Early

2

FRIDAY, 29th MARCH, 1963   7-30 p.m. to 11-15 p.m.

Liverpool's One and Only

Gerry & The Pacemakers

Plus Three Other Top Line Groups

Members 4/6 · Visitors 5/6

3

SUNDAY, 7th APRIL, 1963   7-30 p.m. to 11-15 p.m.

"TWIST 'N' TRAD" SPECIAL

Return Visit of the Sensational

Alan Elsdon Jazz Band

Plus   The Four Mosts   The Swinging Bluegenes

          The Flintstones   The Zenith Six Jazz Band

Members 5/6 · Visitors 6/6

4

GOOD FRIDAY, 12th APRIL, 1963   4 p.m. to Midnight

A Shot of Rhythm & Blues

R & B MARATHON No. 2 STARRING

THE BEATLES

PLUS 8 OTHER GREAT MERSEYSIDE R & B GROUPS

Members 7/6 · Visitors 8/6   Pass Outs Available

Please, Please be Early - 4 o'clock Start

Evening Sessions Sun., Tues., Wed., Fri., & Sat. Every Week

Don't Forget!   There are Swinging Lunchtime Sessions

Featuring Top Rock Groups each Mon., Tues., Wed., Thurs. & Friday

12 noon to 2-15 p.m. Members 1/- Visitors 1/6

AT THE CAVERN CLUB

New Members & Visitors always welcome. Yearly membership fee only 1/-

NOTE: STRICTLY NO ADMISSIONS AFTER 9-30 p.m.

Pete Best's tour itinerary

Starting out on the road

The basement of a 15-room Victorian house in Liverpool was the unlikely home for a club which boasted a coffee bar, jukebox and live bands at the weekends. The Casbah Club was opened during the summer of 1959 by Mona Best, who lived there with her husband John and sons Pete and Rory.

Among the visitors to the club in the weeks before its opening were John Lennon, Paul McCartney and George Harrison and they all lent a hand (together with Cynthia Powell who was later to become Mrs Lennon) in painting the walls in readiness for the official first night on August 29, 1959 when a local band took to the stage as the club's resident group. "It was great to be involved in the birth of a coffee bar," said McCartney. "All of us lent a hand. And after we had painted it up it was our club."

The Quarrymen on that opening night consisted of Harrison, his two mates Lennon and McCartney plus bass player Ken Brown. They stood in for the pre-booked Les Stewart Quartet who pulled out of the booking. The reformed Quarrymen were paid £3 a night and it cost fans a shilling (5p) on top of their annual membership fee of 2/6d (12.5p) to see them throughout September and October 1959 when a row over payments saw Lennon, McCartney and Harrison walk out and give up their residency.

They were replaced by a band called The Blackjacks which featured Mona's son Pete Best on drums and by the time Lennon, McCartney and Harrison returned to the club as visitors in 1960, they had become The Silver Beetles and were in need of a drummer for their debut trip to Hamburg. They set about recruiting Best and on their return from Hamburg the first date the new four-piece played in the UK was at the Casbah Club on December 17, 1960.

Throughout 1961 and into 1962 Mona and Pete Best took charge of booking the Beatles' live appearances and it was in the Casbah coffee bar where the Beatles

– Lennon, McCartney, Harrison and Best – met up with Brian Epstein in December 1961 to discuss the idea of the local record shop owner becoming their manager.

The Beatles played their last show at the Casbah on June 24, 1962 – the club closed down a few days later – but they had already become firm favourites on the live circuit around Lancashire and the north west of England and, according to the note received by Best, the four musicians got the details of their dates in the post from their manager's office. While the appearances listed for July 1962 all went ahead, extra shows were added on the 19th in Birkenhead and at the Cavern the following lunchtime.

(Above) The small stage area inside the Casbah Club.
(Right) Pete Best's date sheet.
(Overleaf) The leather-clad Beatles performing at their first ever show 'down south', when fewer than 20 people turned up to see them at the Palais Ballroom in Aldershot on December 9, 1961.

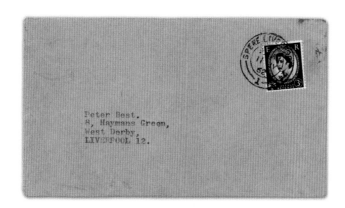

Peter Best.
8, Haymans Green,
West Derby,
LIVERPOOL 12.

THE BEATLES - Bookings July/August etc.

July	9th	Monday	Plaza Ballroom, St. Helens
"	11th	Wednesday	Cavern Club, Liverpool
"	12th	Thursday LT.	Cavern Club
			Majestic Ballroom, New Brighton.
"	13th	Friday	Tower Ballroom, New Brighton
"	14th	Saturday	Regent Ballroom, Rhyl.
"	15th	Sunday	Cavern Club, Liverpool.
"	16th	Monday LT.	Cavern Club.
			Plaza Ballroom, St. Helens
"	17th	Tuesday	Swindon (2 Spots 60 mins. each)
"	18th	Wednesday LT.	Cavern Club.
			Cavern Club.
"	20th	Friday LT.	Cavern Club.
			Bell Hall, Warrington
"	21st	Saturday	Tower Ballroom
"	22nd	Sunday	Cavern Club
"	23rd	Monday	Kingsway Club, Southport.
"	24th	Tuesday LT.	Cavern Club
"	25th	Wednesday LT.	Cavern Club
			Cabaret Club, Duke Street.
"	26th	Thursday	Cambridge Hall, Southport (JOE BROWN SHOW)
"	27th	Friday	Tower Ballroom, New Brighton (JOE BROWN SHOW)
"	28th	Saturday	Cavern Club.
"	30th	Monday	St. Johns
"	31st	Tuesday LT.	Cavern Club.
August	1st	Wednesday	Cavern Club.
"	3rd	Friday	Grafton Rooms Liverpool
	4th	Saturday	Victoria Hall, Higher Bebington

COMING SHORTLY

August	10th	Friday	Riverboat Shuffle (Cavern)
	11th	Saturday	Odd Spot
	18th	Saturday	Hulme Hall, Port Sunlight
	24th	Friday	River Cruise
	25th	Saturday	Marine Hall Ballroom, Fleetwood
	31st	Friday	Lydney
Sept.	1st	Saturday	Stroud
	15th	Saturday	Northwich
	22nd	Saturday	Majestic Ballroom, Birkenhead.
	28th	Friday	River Cruise
Oct.	6th	Saturday	Golden Primrose Restaurant, Port Sunlight

N.B. Watch the weekly details lists for cancellations and
insertions.

George's Gretch
George and his guitars

In his first year as a teenager, George Harrison got a kidney inflammation and, as he lay in his hospital bed, he got an urge to own a guitar. It was while he was recovering in Alder Hey Hospital in Liverpool that the young Harrison decided to follow in his dad's footsteps and start playing the guitar. Fortunately he knew that a school friend had one for sale.

"I heard that Raymond Hughes had a guitar he wanted to sell for £3 10s. It was a lot of money then but my mum gave me the money and I went to Raymond's house and bought it," recalls Harrison who, inspired by the likes of Eddie Cochran and Lonnie Donegan soon moved on to his "first decent guitar". Armed with his Hofner President, which he made semi-electric with the addition of a pick-up, Harrison toured with Lennon and McCartney in both the Quarrymen and Johnny and the Moondogs, but along the way swapped his Hofner President for a Hofner Club 40, owned by a member of rival group the Swinging Blue Jeans.

From there Harrison moved on to get a genuine electric guitar all of his own and, although he would have preferred an American Fender Stratocaster, he had to make do with an alternative model made in Eastern Europe. "If I'd had my way the Strat would have been my first guitar. I'd seen Buddy Holly's Strat ... but in Liverpool in those days the only thing I could find resembling a Strat was a Futurama."

In fact, American guitars of any kind were hard to find in the years following World War II, due to a ban on importing goods from America. Harrison was forced to stop off at Frank Hessy's music store in November 1959 and buy a Czech-made Resonet Futurama for just over £50.

By 1963 Harrison had added at least two Gretsch guitars (a Jet Firebird and a Duo-Jet) to his collection and in May he bought a third Gretsch, the Country Gentleman guitar as designed by one of his all-time heroes Chet Atkins. The Beatles' manager Brian Epstein

had arranged a deal with the London music store Sound City and Harrison visited the store off Shaftesbury Avenue to be fitted for his new guitar, which was listed in Sound City adverts as costing £264.

Later Harrison bought a second slightly updated Gretsch Country Gentleman guitar and continued to use Gretsches on stage rather than in the studio. A photograph of him playing one was used in Gretsch promotional material.

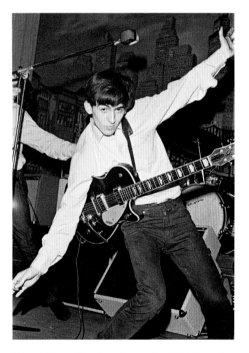

(Above) George Harrison shows off with his favourite Gretsch Duo-Jet guitar.

(Right) The second-hand Gretsch guitar that Harrison used regularly on stage and in the studio in the early 1960s.

Ringo's drums
A Premier set for £125

Although he was the last to join the Liverpool quartet who went on to become world beaters, Ringo Starr began his love affair with drums in the mid-1950s after seeing the film *Rock Around the Clock*, starring Bill Haley and his Rockets.

"My first kit came on the scene about this time," recalls Ringo. "I bought a drum for 30 shillings. It was a huge one-sided bass drum." Already fascinated by rock 'n' roll and teddy boys, Starr eventually got hold of a drum kit as a Christmas present and moved into skiffle with his first band the Eddie Clayton Skiffle Group, which he formed with a bunch of co-workers.

When he joined local Liverpool group Rory Storm and the Hurricanes, Starr borrowed £46 from his grandfather and armed himself with an early Ajax single-headed drum kit. From there he moved on to the Premier drum kit which was with him when he was recruited into the Beatles on August 18, 1962, and throughout their first recordings sessions for EMI and on to their debut album *Please Please Me*.

Starr bought his Premier Model 54 drum kit during the summer of 1960 for a hefty £125. For his money he got a bass drum, rack tom, floor tom, a wood-shell snare drum and Zyn cymbals mounted on Premier stands. The whole thing came in what Premier dubbed as a Duroplastic 'mahogany'-coloured finish and was advertised in their brochure as the drum kit for "the busy modern group; for the recording drummer who is looking for the sharpest response and fidelity of tone."

Premier had begun making drums in the UK in 1922 under the direction of drummer Albert Della Porta and drum-builder George Smith. Based in central London, they moved to Acton in the 1930s and eventually to Leicester after World War II. By the end of the 1970s – in addition to Ringo Starr and a 1966 Queen's Award to Industry – they had on their roll call customers such as Nick Mason, Phil Collins, Brian Bennett, Keith Moon, Carl Palmer, Bill Bruford and John Bonham.

In his days with the Hurricanes, Starr put his R S initials on the bass drum, although some thought they also stood for the band's leader Rory Storm. However, later on, as he became better known, he had the name Ringo Starr emblazoned on to the bass drum.

The Premier kit was the one that Starr took with him to Abbey Road studios when the Beatles recorded their first single 'Love Me Do' on September 4, 1962, although producer George Martin used session drummer Andy White on a later September 11 session as, according to fellow EMI producer Ron Richards, "We weren't happy with the drum sound on the original."

Reduced to playing tambourine on the second session, Starr commented, "I was devastated that George Martin had his doubts about me", but he continued to play his Premier drum kit until he upgraded to a Ludwig set in 1963.

(Right) Ringo Starr's Premier 54 drum kit, which he used during the Beatles' first recording sessions at Abbey Road studios in September 1962.

John Lennon's glasses

Rebel style

After his parents separated in 1945, John Lennon, aged just five, moved into Mendips, a semi-detached house belonging to his Aunt Mimi and Uncle George Smith. "I was a nice clean-cut suburban boy. We owned our own house, had our own garden," was Lennon's description of his new childhood home.

Mendips was in fact number 25 Menlove Avenue in the Woolton area of Liverpool and it was in the front porch of the house, below Lennon's small bedroom, that he and McCartney sat and practised with their acoustic guitars. "There was a good acoustic, like a bathroom acoustic, and it was the only place Mimi would let us make noise," recalled McCartney who also remembered the times they sat in Lennon's bedroom.

"Then we'd go up to John's room and we'd sit on the bed and play records. It's a wonderful memory," he said before recounting how the song 'I Call Your Name' was written there. "Physically it was always a bad idea to sit side by side on the bed in his bedroom. The necks of our guitars were always banging. We worked on it together but it was John's idea."

Mendips was also the place where 'Please Please Me' began to take shape as Lennon recounted. "It was my attempt at writing a Roy Orbison song. I remember the day I wrote it. I remember the pink eiderdown over the bed, sitting in one of the bedrooms in my house on Menlove Avenue" and he also explained that another song came from a local bus journey. "It started out on a bus journey from my house on 251, Menlove Avenue to town. I had a complete set of lyrics, naming every sight. It became 'In My Life', a remembrance of friends and lovers of the past."

It was also outside his home that Lennon's mother Julia was knocked down and killed as she ran to catch a bus at the Menlove Avenue stop on July 15, 1958.

While the National Trust was apparently reluctant to purchase Mendips – they assumed that no Beatle songs were ever composed there – Lennon's widow Yoko Ono bought it and donated it to the National Trust, saying, "I wanted to preserve it for the people of Liverpool and John Lennon and the Beatles' fans all over the world."

After extensive restoration, the house was opened to the public in March 2003 – with an appropriate blue plaque – and given Grade II listed building status. It remains a major tourist attraction.

Brit pop band Oasis paid tribute to Lennon and Mendips by featuring the house on the cover of their single 'Live Forever', while band member Noel Gallagher emphasized his admiration for songwriter, singer and guitarist by opting for round, wire-framed tinted glasses similar to those worn by Lennon.

(Left) The fashionable blue-tinted prescription glasses worn by John Lennon – and later by both Liam and Noel Gallagher of Oasis.

(Right) Notoriously poor-sighted John Lennon took to wearing round-framed 'granny' glasses during the swinging sixties.

20 Forthlin Road, Liverpool
Where Paul grew up

Remembering the family home where he grew up in from the age of 13, Paul McCartney said, "We'd go to my house because there really wasn't anywhere else. We'd both have acoustic guitars and we'd sit opposite each other and play"

The house was number 20 Forthlin Road in the Allerton district of Liverpool and it was home to McCartney, his mother and father and brother Mike from 1955 although Mrs McCartney died the year after they moved in.

The small terraced house was built in the 1920s by the local council and was one of the first places where McCartney and his long-time song-writing partner Lennon worked on their earliest compositions. Skipping off school, the two of them would go to the house and while Lennon waited at the front door, McCartney climbed up a drainpipe, got in through an open toilet window and then let his partner in together with their guitars.

"I would sag off school and John would get off art college and we would sit down with our two guitars and plonk away. We wrote songs together. I wrote them down in an exercise book and above them it always said 'Another Lennon/McCartney original'." explained McCartney. Among the 'originals' created in the small front room of the Forthlin Road house were 'I Saw Her Standing There' and 'Love Me Do' – "one of us would come up with an idea and then it would see-saw" recalled McCartney while 'Let It Be' and 'When I'm Sixty-Four' were also conceived in the house.

One of the McCartney's neighbours in Forthlin Road was a tailor and he made an early set of stage clothes – five lilac jackets – for the Beatles when they first went to Hamburg in 1960. "We picked out some material ourselves and took it to him to make jackets. The others came to my house for fittings."

The McCartney family home was also where McCartney's brother Mike – using the name McGear – met with Roger McGough and John Gorman as they created the Scaffold. As the Beatles became more and more successful, fans descended on the house and camped outside in the road. Eventually the McCartney family were forced to move out and Paul McCartney, who moved to London, bought his father a new home 25 miles away from Forthlin Road which was eventually purchased by the National Trust in 1995 for £55,000. They spent a further £47,000 refurbishing the property before opening it to the public as "the birthplace of the Beatles" in 1998, but because McCartney is still alive the house doesn't qualify for a National Trust 'blue plaque'.

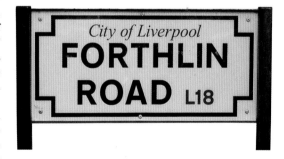

(Above) The road sign of the Liverpool street in which Paul McCartney lived during the fifties and sixties.

(Right) Paul McCartney's childhood home, where he met with John Lennon and created some of the earliest Beatles' songs.

Kaiserkeller contract

On to the king's cellar

With Hamburg's Indra Club closed down, the Beatles, who had a contract with local promoter Bruno Koschmider which included a clause forbidding them from playing in any other venue within 40 kilometres of the city, were swiftly moved into another club run by the German businessman.

Despite not being into music – "Bruno wasn't some young rock 'n' roll entrepreneur … and he didn't seem to know much about music" commented Harrison – the former circus clown and fire eater was at the heart of Hamburg's thriving club scene and on October 4, 1960 he moved the Beatles into the Kaiserkeller with its huge stage which they shared with fellow Liverpool band Rory Storm and the Hurricanes throughout an eight-week booking. "The Kaiserkeller was great – at least it had a dance floor," was Harrison's opinion of the group's new venue.

During this time the Beatles' following increased with locals buying them beer and urging them sing American rock 'n' roll while the group took to cavorting about the huge stage under the influence of alcohol and pep pills, imitating the crippled rock star Gene Vincent and even giving Heil Hitler salutes. "We had to play for hours and hours on end", recounted Lennon. "Every song lasted twenty minutes and had twenty solos in it. We'd be playing eight or ten hours a night. That's what improved the playing."

The Beatles and the Hurricanes also shared a bet to see which group could smash the club's rotting stage and it was Rory Storm who finally put his foot through the boards and incurred a 65DM fine from Koschmider to pay for the damage.

Booked to appear at the Kasierkeller Hamburg through until the end of 1960, the Beatles began to forge plans to move on to another club in 1961; but when Koschmider heard they were looking to appear at the nearby rival Top Ten Club, he reminded them that they could not play at any other venue in the city without his permission. Despite this warning, the group began to spend more time at the Top Ten Club including jumping on stage to jam with English singer Tony Sheridan.

When he heard the news Koschmider decided to terminate the Beatles contract (and Rory Storm's) while at the same time the local authorities somehow discovered that Harrison was only 17 and, under West German law, forbidden from attending a night club after midnight … let alone playing there in a rock 'n' roll group. Koschmider sent a note to Harrison and the Beatles on November 1 giving notice that they had to leave by November 30.

Harrison in fact left Germany on November 21, 1960 while Lennon, McCartney, Best and Sutcliffe stayed on to complete the series of bookings but their 58 night residency at the Kaiserkeller ended on November 30 when McCartney and Best were also deported, accused of arson after they had set light to some wallpaper in their one-room 'home' at the Bambi Kino.

(Right) A 1960 poster showing the Beatles below Rory Storm (and his Hurican) during their three-month stint at the Kaiserkeller.

(Overleaf) Club owner Bruno Koschmider's Kaiserkeller contract, detailing the Beatles' playing time and featuring a hand-written reference to the rival Top Ten Club, where the Beatles moved on to in 1961.

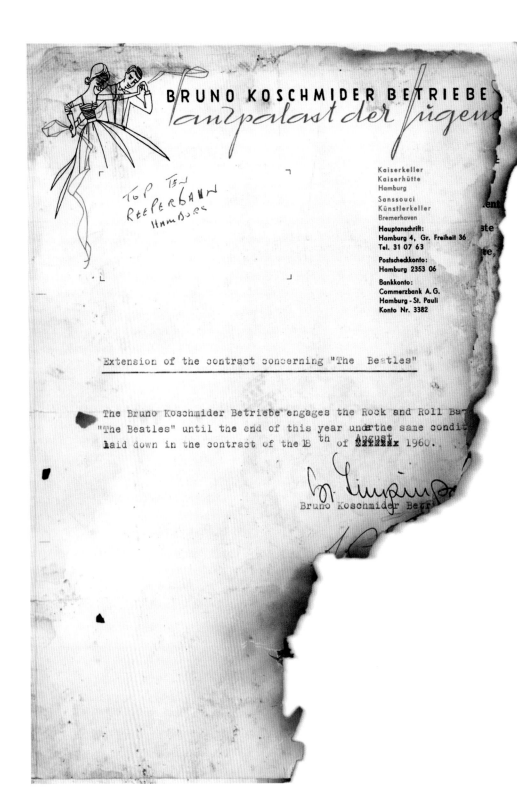

BRUNO KOSCHMIDER BETRIEBE

Tanzpalast der Jugend

TOP TEN
REEPERBAHN
HAMBURG

Kaiserkeller
Kaiserhütte
Hamburg

Sanssouci
Künstlerkeller
Bremerhaven

Hauptanschrift:
Hamburg 4, Gr. Freiheit 36
Tel. 31 07 63

Postscheckkonto:
Hamburg 2353 06

Bankkonto:
Commerzbank A.G.
Hamburg - St. Pauli
Konto Nr. 3382

Extension of the contract concerning "The Beatles"

The Bruno Koschmider Betriebe engages the Rock and Roll Ba
"The Beatles" until the end of this year under the same condit
laid down in the contract of the 18 th of August 1960.

Bruno Koschmider Be

ADDITIONAL CLAUSES

1) Should ~~either~~ The Beatles break the contracht they will
   compensate Mr. Koschmider in full

2) Should Mr. Koschmider break the contract he will be held
   liable to pay the full fee of engagement for tour.

3) Mr. Koschmider to set working permits for The Beatles.

PLAYING TIMES

~~Tue~~sday to Friday playing times 41/2 hours
   pm to 9-30 pm, break 1/2 hour. 10-00 pm to 11-00 pm break 1/2 hour
1-30 to 12-30 am break 1/2 hour. 1 00 am to 2 am.

~~Sa~~turday playing times 6 hours
~~7~~00 pm to 8-30 pm break 1/2 hour. 9-00 pm to 10-00 pm break 1/2 hour
~~10~~-30 pm to 11-30 pm break 1/2 hour. 12-00 to 1-00 am break 1/2 hour
~~1~~30 am to 3 00 am.
h
~~Sun~~day playing times 6 houres
   pm to 6-00 pm break 1/2 hour. 6-30 to 7-30 pm 1/2 hour break.
~~8-30~~ to 9-00 pm break 1/2 hour. 9-30 to 10-30 pm break 1/2 hour.
~~11~~ to 12.00 pm break 1/2 hour. 12-30 to 1-30 am
~~Con~~
~~half~~
~~Musi~~ agree to aside to the conditions laid out in
~~abo~~ve contract.

John Lennon's Rickenbacker

The guitar of his dreams

Like his mates in the Beatles, John Lennon's first flirtation with an instrument came when he was a teenager in Liverpool and discovered rock 'n' roll. "I had no idea about doing music as a way of life until rock 'n' roll hit me. That's the music that inspired me to play," was his recollection. And it was after his mother Julia had taught him to play the banjo that the young Lennon ordered his first guitar from a magazine advertisement and had it sent to his mother's address.

Who actually paid the £10 remains unclear, but it was in around 1954 that Lennon took possession of a Gallotone Champion Spanish guitar. "It was a bit crummy but I played it all the time and got a lot of practice," he said and adopting a style which involved him playing his guitar like a banjo, Lennon learnt early rock classics, such as 'Ain't That a Shame' and 'That'll Be The Day'.

A few years later Lennon's Aunt Mimi, who he was now living with, splashed out a £17 deposit on a new Club 40 Hofner guitar from Hessy's musical instrument shop in the Whitechapel district of Liverpool. With a further £23 to pay in instalments, she gave it to the aspiring young musician with the warning, "The guitar's all right as a hobby, but you'll never make a living from it."

After using the guitar during performances with the Quarrymen, Johnny and the Moondogs, the Silver Beetles and finally the Beatles, Lennon moved on to find the guitar of his dreams in 1960. The Rickenbacker 325 Capri model was launched by the American instrument company Ro-Pat-In Corporation, founded in California in 1931.

Rickenbacker was the brand name the company introduced after they added electric and bass guitars to their original range of Hawaiian guitars. The 325 Capri series was introduced in 1958, when the post World War II ban on American goods being imported into the UK was still in place.

Lennon was in Germany during the Beatles' run of 106 dates in the clubs of Hamburg – between August and November 1960 – when he came across the Rickenbacker guitar in either the Selmer store or Musikhaus Rotthoff. At the time they sold in America for around $270 (the equivalent of £100) but all Lennon recalled was "I bought it in Germany on HP. I remember that whatever it cost, it was a hell of a lot of money to me at the time."

For the next four years Lennon took his Rickenbacker on the road and into the recording studios with the Beatles and even went as far as describing it as "the most beautiful guitar ... the action is ridiculously low."

When Lennon, who had heard US musician Toots Thielemans play a Rickenbacker in the George Shearing Quintet, bought the guitar, it was finished with a body in natural alder, but he had it re-finished in black and added a vibrato tailpiece as well as moving the control knobs.

In fact, in a 1965 interview Lennon included the guitar among his most prized possessions, perhaps knowing that by that time an original late 1958 Rickenbacker 325 was a rare guitar and a much sought-after collector's item.

(Left) John Lennon on stage with his 'beautiful' Rickenbacker guitar.

(Right) The American Rickenbacker guitar that John Lennon bought on hire purchase in Germany in late 1960.

George's leather jacket
The rock 'n' roll look

Sometime in 1961 the Beatles adopted a new stage outfit – black leather trousers and black leather jackets worn over a black t-shirt. According to Harrison it was a fashion they adopted after first spotting leather trousers during their trips to play in Hamburg in the early 1960s. "And then we saw those leather pants and we thought 'wow we've got to get some of them'."

With the help of band member Sutcliffe's girlfriend Astrid Kirchherr, all four band members soon had a pair of black leather trousers made for them by a German tailor and they then added American cowboy boots to the outfit which was topped off by the t-shirt and jacket plus a strange pink cap which they dubbed 'twat hats'. "That became our band uniform", explained Harrison, "cowboy boots, twat hats and black leather suits."

Lennon's opinion of the Beatles new uniform was that "we looked like four Gene Vincents – only a bit younger." Certainly American rock 'n' roll singer Vincent was a major influence on the Beatles mainly through his recordings of 'Ain't She Sweet' and 'Be Bop A Lula' – two songs the Beatles included in their earliest stage shows – but also through his preference for leather outfits which had become popular with motor-cycle-riding rockers.

However, when Epstein took over as manager of the Beatles in January 1962, the group's 'leather look' came under close scrutiny with Lennon admitting, "Outside of Liverpool, when we went down south in our leather outfits, the dance hall promoters didn't really like us. They thought we looked like a gang of thugs", and Harrison adding, "With black t-shirts, black leather gear and sweaty we did look like hooligans."

Even though he had reservations Epstein still had the group photographed in their leather outfits for their first professional session – by Liverpool photographer Albert Marrion – and he used the shot as a publicity picture to promote the band. But things began to change soon as the manager declared, "I first encouraged them to get out of leather jackets and I wouldn't allow them to appear in jeans after a short time" and it seems that nobody in the group was particularly concerned about the change of image, particularly as it brought more work.

"We gladly switched into suits to get some more money and some more gigs", explained Harrison while McCartney added, "That started to change the image and, though we would still were leather occasionally, for the posh do's we'd put on suits." Having abandoned the 'hard' image of the all leather outfits, the Beatles followed Epstein's advice and switched to smarter outfits which would get them more work – a move acknowledged by McCartney as "something of an end to the Hamburg era."

(Above) The Beatles on stage at the Cavern in 1961.

(Right) George Harrison's jacket, which was part of the Beatles' outfit of the time – 'cowboy hats, twat hats and black leather suits' – which he thought made them look like 'hooligans'.

Payslip from the Top Ten Club

The third Hamburg venue

Just before they were deported back to the UK at the end of November 1960, the Beatles managed to negotiate a new deal which would enable them to return to Hamburg during the following year. Having met Top Ten Club owner Peter Eckhorn before their sudden and unscheduled return to Liverpool, they agreed a one-month booking in April 1961 – subject to them being allowed back into Germany.

Originally a topless circus run by Eckhorn's father under the name The Hippodrome, the Top Ten Club opened as a music venue in October 1960 in the famous Reeperbahn, with Eckhorn junior booking Tony Sheridan and the Jets as the main attraction. However, he was sufficiently impressed by the Beatles during their impromptu performances with Sheridan to add them to the bill.

The new Beatles' contract, negotiated without any help from their earlier booking agent Allan Williams, required them to appear from March 27 through to July 2, but Eckhorn had first to negotiate with the West German authorities to get McCartney and Best allowed back into the country. After the Top Ten Club owner had paid 158DM – the cost of their two fares back to the UK the previous November – the bass player and the drummer were granted permission to return, and as Harrison had turned 18 in February 1961, he was also able to return and join the group.

After the Beatles returned to the UK in December 1960, Sutcliffe had chosen to remain in Hamburg with his new girlfriend Astrid Kirchherr, to focus on his art. With his involvement with the Beatles at an end, Sutcliffe was given the job of informing Williams that the Beatles believed that they had made the Top Ten Club booking without his help and were therefore not going to pay him his commission.

According to the pay slip, it seems that club owner Eckhorn paid the four Beatles and Tony Sheridan on a weekly basis – which meant they each netted 215DM after 30DM had been deducted – and they all had had to sign the pay sheet.

Playing from 7pm until 2am with a 15-minute break every hour, The Beatles quickly strengthened their stage act and increased their following. "We performed like a gang of lunatics. It was alright once we got the hang of it all and it was great fun", recalls Harrison, while McCartney explained, "In a way it was marvellous simply because we could experiment." It was during their residency at the Top Ten Club that Sutcliffe finally left the group and handed over duties as the group's bass player to McCartney.

(Above) John Lennon on stage at the Top Ten Club in 1961.

(Right) The pay slip for the five members of the Beatles and Tony Sheridan, who shared a total of 1,290DM for a week's work at the Top Ten Club.

Musiker - Gehälter v. 15. - 21. 4. 61   248

Georg Harrison   7 Tage à 35.- = DM 245,-
  i. à uo. Lohn - u. Kirchensteuer   "   30.-   215,-
          George Harrison.

Paul Mc. Cartney   7 Tage à 35.- = DM 245,-
  i. à uo. Lohn - u. Kirchensteuer   "   30.-   215,-
          Paul McCartney.

John Lennon   7 Tage à 35.- = DM 245,-
  i. à uo. Lohn - u. Kirchensteuer   "   30.-   215,-

          J W. Lennon.

Stuart Sutcliffe   7 Tage à 35.- = DM 245,-
  i. à uo. Lohn - u. Kirchensteuer   "   30.-   215,-

          StuSutcliffe..

Peter Best   7 Tage à 35.- = DM 245,-
  i. à uo. Lohn - u. Kirchensteuer   "   30.-   215,-
          Peter Best

Tony Sheridan   7 Tage à 35.- = DM 245,-
  i. à uo. Lohn - u. Kirchensteuer   "   30.-   215,-
                                    TonySheridan

                                    1 290,-

Paul's Hofner bass

The 'violin' guitar

Still recognized today as the left-handed bass player with the most famous group in the world, Paul McCartney's introduction to his fellow Beatle John Lennon was as a promising guitar player who knew the chords and all the words to Eddie Cochran's 'Twenty Flight Rock'.

It was way back in 1957 when McCartney joined the Quarrymen who over the next few year progressed to become the Silver Beetles and finally the Beatles by which time Harrison, Best and Sutcliffe were also on board with Sutcliffe lining up as the bass player. And it was only following his decision to remain in Germany after the group's debut club appearances in Hamburg in 1960 that the group began to seek a new bass player.

After a brief period with Chas Newby on bass, it seems that McCartney took on the role in early 1961 but only after Harrison had declined an invitation from Lennon to switch from lead guitar. Armed at first with Sutcliffe's Hofner 333 bass, which he had to turn upside down to play, McCartney eventually sought out a bass guitar of his own and decided to stay with the make he had inherited.

Hofner were founded in Germany in 1887 and had traded as successful manufacturers of string instruments for nearly 70 years before they created their hollow-bodied violin shaped Hofner 500/1 electric bass guitar for the Frankfurt Music Fair in 1956. It was one of these which McCartney turned to in 1961 when the Beatles were performing in Hamburg.

"I found a nice little shop in the centre of Hamburg ... I saw this bass in the window, this violin-shaped bass, the Hofner," he said. Taken with its shape – which when the left-handed McCartney turned it upside down remained symmetrical – the young musician purchased the guitar from the shop and although a shop assistant from the time reckons it was paid for in instalments, McCartney has a different recollection. "I paid for it outright. It was equivalent of about 30 quid which was pretty cheap even back then."

There is also conjecture that McCartney's first Hofner bass was in fact custom-made for him as left-handed guitars of any sort were in short supply in the early 1960s. Either way the Hofner 500/1 violin bass quickly became a feature of the Beatles' appearances both at home and abroad and was soon dubbed both the 'Beatles bass' and the 'Cavern bass'. In McCartney's own words, it was the start of wonderful relationship – "That was it; it was the start of what became a kind of trademark."

In 1963 McCartney was given a second 500/1 bass by Hofner which he used on the *With The Beatles* album and also throughout the Beatles' touring years until they 'retired' from live work in 1966. It's been claimed that his original Hofner bass was stolen during the shooting of the film *Let It Be* and McCartney had to use his later 1963 model – which he has continued to use throughout his solo concerts and recordings – during the group's legendary live session on the roof of their Savile Row offices.

(Right) Paul McCartney's favourite Hofner bass guitar, which cost him around £30 in 1961 and became 'a kind of trademark'.

(Overleaf) Paul McCartney tuning his Hofner bass guitar during an Abbey Road recording session in July 1963.

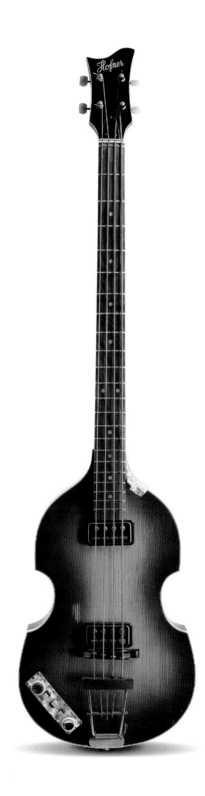

'My Bonnie'
The Beatles' first recording

By the time German producer Bert Kaempfert got the idea to record Tony Sheridan, the British singer was no longer backed by his group the Jets and was being accompanied during his shows at Hamburg's Top Ten Club by an assortment of groups and musicians – including the Beatles.

Once they had returned to Germany in March 1961, the group backed Sheridan more than once as Harrison recalled. "We were backing up lots of people at the Top Ten. The singer Tony Sheridan was there ... and we used to back him. He was older than us as well and was more hardened to the business whereas we just getting into it, more bouncy and naïve."

Kampfert and his band had topped the US charts in January 1961 with his instrumental theme to the film *Wonderland By Night* and in August of the same year 'Wooden Heart' – a song he co-wrote – was another American number one for Joe Dowell. At the same time he was also employed by the German record company Polydor as a producer and, in an effort to make rock and pop records, he signed Sheridan to the label.

Because he had no backing band of his own, Sheridan suggested to the producer that his friends the Beatles should be hired to join him on the recording sessions which, despite some differing suggestions over dates, seem to have taken place on June 22 and 23, 1961 in the Harburg Friedrich Ebert Halle. With Sutcliffe out of the band and McCartney on bass, the Beatles received a flat fee with no royalties to back Sheridan as he sang 'My Bonnie', 'The Saints' and 'Why'.

However, when it came to releasing the single in Germany, Kaempfert had some concerns over the name the Beatles as it sounded remarkably like the German word for penis – *Peedles* – and opted to change the name of the group. "It was actually Tony Sheridan *und die* Beat Brothers," recalls McCartney. "They didn't like our name and said 'Change to The Beat Brothers, this is more understandable for the German audience'. We went along with it – it was a record."

And despite Lennon's unfavourable view of the record – "It's just Tony Sheridan singing with us banging in the background. It's terrible. It could be anybody" – the single rose to number 32 in the German charts where it remained for 12 weeks and, according to the producer, sold over 100,000 copies. It was eventually released in the UK in 1963 – when it was credited to 'Tony Sheridan & the Beatles' – and reached number 48 in the charts.

Perhaps as some sort of favour, Kaempfert allowed the Beatles to use the last hour of the session in June 1961 to record a couple of numbers without Sheridan. They chose 'Ain't She Sweet' and an instrumental written by John and George called 'Cry For A Shadow', but they still failed to get any recognition although they were offered and signed a one-year recording deal – from May 1961 – with the German record producer.

(Right) Two years after being released in Germany, 'My Bonnie' was issued in the UK in 1963, with a credit for the Beatles.

(Overleaf) George Harrison (left) and John Lennon doing their job as backing musicians for singer Tony Sheridan in Hamburg, Germany in 1961.

Brian Epstein's diary

Two days in June

Brian Epstein had a shop called NEMS ... and we bought all our records there." That's how McCartney described the man who launched and guided the Beatles' career during the group's most successful years. Taking over management in early 1962, Epstein went from record shop owner to global entrepreneur, as he negotiated record, film, publishing and performance deals for the most famous group in the world.

In the late 1950s Epstein's family ran a furniture store in Walton Road, Liverpool which also sold sheet music and pianos. One of their customers had been McCartney's father Jim, who according to McCartney "bought his first piano from Harry Epstein [Brian's father]". Later, Brian was involved in the family's expansion into the electrical business as they opened a store in Great Charlotte Street where he took charge of the record department.

The next move was to a central Liverpool site in Whitechapel where Epstein managed the second NEMS (North End Music Stores) record shop which was opened by star singer Anthony Newley. The shop quickly became a success with Epstein cleverly assessing the sort of records teenagers in Liverpool wanted to buy – and among his customers were hopeful young musicians such as McCartney. "It [NEMS] was quite a gathering place; one of the shops where you could find the records you wanted."

It was the NEMS store in Charlotte Street that Raymond Jones walked into in October 1961 in search of a record called 'My Bonnie' by a group named the Beatles. Epstein didn't have it in stock but after some detective work tracked it down to Germany, ordered a box of 25 copies and put a sign in the shop window saying "Beatles Record Available". When Bill Harry launched his *Mersey Beat* magazine in July 1961, NEMS was among the local stores who took copies and slowly Epstein became aware of the growing interest in the local 'beat scene' and one band in particular – the Beatles.

After he visited the nearby Cavern Club in November 1961, Epstein's enthusiasm for the group became even greater and eventually he invited the group to his office above the NEMS store for a meeting. "One evening we went down to the NEMS shop", recalled McCartney. "We went up to Brian's office to make the deal. I was talking to him, trying to beat him down, knowing the game; try to get the manager to take a low percentage."

However Epstein stuck to his guns and demanded a 25% cut of the group's income in return for his expertise and assistance and it was a deal that the Beatles eventually agreed to. "He stuck at a figure of 25%. He told us 'That'll do, now I'll be your manager' and we agreed. With my dad's advice – I remember dad had said to get a Jewish manager – and it all fitted and Brian Epstein became our manager," recalled McCartney.

The deal between Epstein and the Beatles – first agreed in the NEMS shop – took effect from February 1, 1962 and ran for five years during which time Epstein launched NEMS Enterprises, with his brother Clive as a partner, and eventually moved his whole NEMS empire to London, employing over 80 people by 1966.

Looking at Epstein's diary during the heady days of 'Beatlemania', entries for two pages covering June 6 and 7, 1963 – when the group were in the midst of their third nationwide British tour with US star Roy Orbison – suggest that he met with sacked drummer Pete Best, dealt with a matter involving George Martin and had a deal in mind for the forthcoming *Beatles Monthly* magazine. The entry "Re Meet The Beatles" (12.30 on Friday June 7) is interesting, as this was the title of first Beatles' album issued by Capitol in America – but not until January 1964.

(Above right) Part of the 1963 diary kept by the Beatles manager Brian Epstein, covering two days in June.

(Below right) Brian Epstein's business card, 1961.

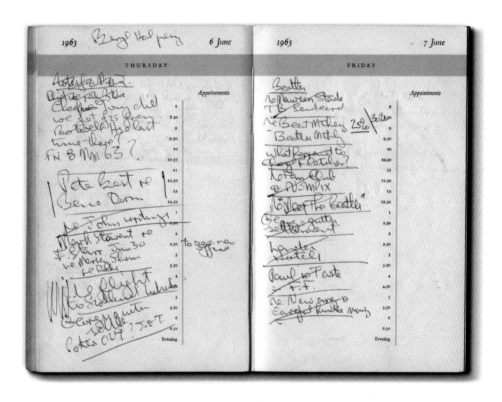

The
Beatles

Business & Personal Manager:
BRIAN EPSTEIN
12-14 WHITECHAPEL
LIVERPOOL 1
ROYal 7895

(Right) July 1966 and Brian Epstein (right) and the Beatles arrive back in Britain from their trip to Japan and the Philippines.

Magnetic hair game

Mop tops

Throughout their days early in Liverpool and on into the clubs of Hamburg, the Beatles had happily sported the rock 'n' roll hairstyle worn by Teddy Boys and their rock idols such as Elvis Presley, Eddie Cochran and Buddy Holly. It was worn with the front turned into a quiff – thanks to a lot of grease – and the back formed into what was called a DA – the 'duck's arse' look.

Band member Sutcliffe was the first to change from this style when girlfriend Astrid Kirchherr seemingly tired of his greasy rocker look. She "brushed it all down, snipped bits off and tidied it up". After suffering a couple of nights of ribbing, first Harrison and then McCartney adopted the same style while Lennon took a while to be persuaded. Best refused to change and maintained his Teddy Boy look until the day he left the Beatles.

A counter-claim to the idea of Sutcliffe's influential girlfriend actually cutting the band's hair into the new style came from German student Jurgen Vollmer who befriended the Beatles in Hamburg and knew both Sutcliffe and Kirchherr. Along with Klaus Voorman, who created the cover artwork for the Beatles' *Revolver* album, photographer Vollmer had adopted the swept-forward fringe style and he suggests that after he moved to Paris in 1960, Lennon and McCartney visited him and decided to adopt his style. "I gave them both their first 'Beatles' haircut in my hotel on the Left Bank," he said.

The group's new hairstyle became generally accepted and it wasn't until they did their first interview with a London newspaper that new haircuts got a mention. Maureen Cleave, writing in the *Evening Standard* made mention of their "weird hair; French styling with the fringe brushed forwards". It was apparently called a French cut although German teenagers had worn it for years while in Sweden it was referred to as a 'Hamlet'.

By the time the Beatles got to America in 1964 the style caused a sensation and the group were dubbed the 'Moptops' after the *New York Times* described the look as "a mop top effect that covers the forehead". Magazines offered hints on to how achieve 'Beatle Hairdos' and a games' makers came up with a novel way of whiling away the evenings, 'wig-mania' also took off in the US with newspapers and radio stations running competitions involving readers and listeners drawing people in a 'Beatlewig' and wig makers churning out hundreds of thousands of 'Beatlewigs' for sale across America.

(Above) A magazine inspired by the Beatles 'French cut' hair style.

(Right) This Beatles magnetic hair game was made in England under licence from NEMS and featured the group's early beetle bug logo.

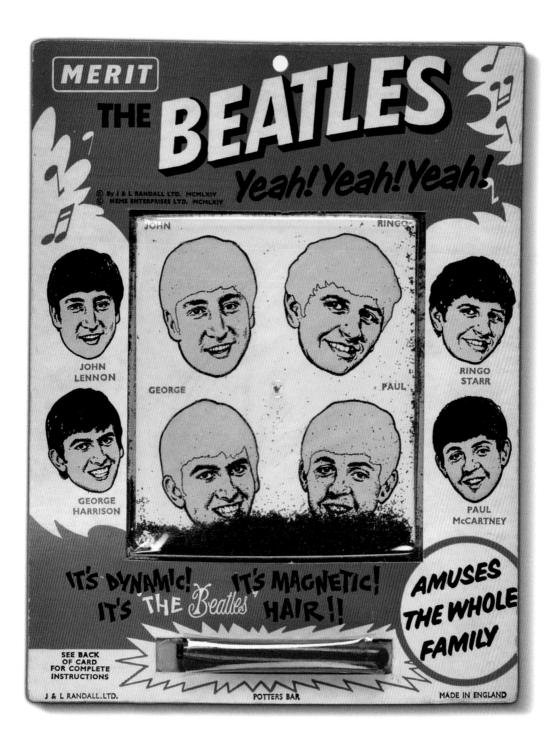

Ringo's postcard

Wish you were here

By the time Ringo Starr sent his postcard from Hamburg on November 14, 1962 to Roy Trafford at his home in Paulton Street, Liverpool 8, the Beatles had both shared the stage and become friends with two of their greatest musical influences – Gene Vincent and Little Richard.

They arrived in Hamburg on November 1, 1962 for a series of shows over 14 nights at the city's Star Club which was the third venue they had played in since their debut in Germany in August 1960. Although they didn't share the bill with the American rock 'n' roll singer, they obviously once again met up with Little Richard as Starr cheekily described him as 'fat'.

Earlier the same year the Beatles had spent seven weeks playing at the same venue in Hamburg and during two of those weeks they appeared alongside Little Richard; although it's unlikely that they performed any of his songs in their set, despite the fact that numbers such as 'Good Golly Miss Molly', 'Long Tall Sally', 'Lucille' and 'Tutti Fruiti' all featured regularly in the Beatles stage act at the time.

Just before the group left for their November dates at the Star Club, they had supported Little Richard both at the Tower Ballroom in New Brighton on October 12 and at the Empire Theatre in Liverpool on October 28 and the American singer told a journalist, "Man, those Beatles are fabulous. If I hadn't seen them I'd never have dreamed they were white. They have a real authentic negro sound."

Gene Vincent was another US rock artist who influenced the Beatles and way before they ever shared a stage, John Lennon, Paul McCartney, George Harrison and Stu Sutcliffe had all been to see him at the Liverpool Stadium in May 1960. And even before then the Beatles – under the names Johnny & the Moondogs and the Silver Beetles – were regularly performing their own versions of Vincent's hit songs such as 'Ain't She Sweet', 'Be-Bop-A-Lula' and 'Over The Rainbow'. It was during their stint at the Star Club – through April and May 1962 – when they got to appear alongside Vincent who commented, "I had a nice band backing me up. They're called the Beatles."

On July 1, 1962, Vincent made a one-off appearance at the Cavern Club in Liverpool where he shared the stage with the Beatles who appeared in matching black leather jackets alongside their hero.

(Right) Ringo Starr's postcard sent to Liverpool from Hamburg in 1962, describing the weather and Little Richard.

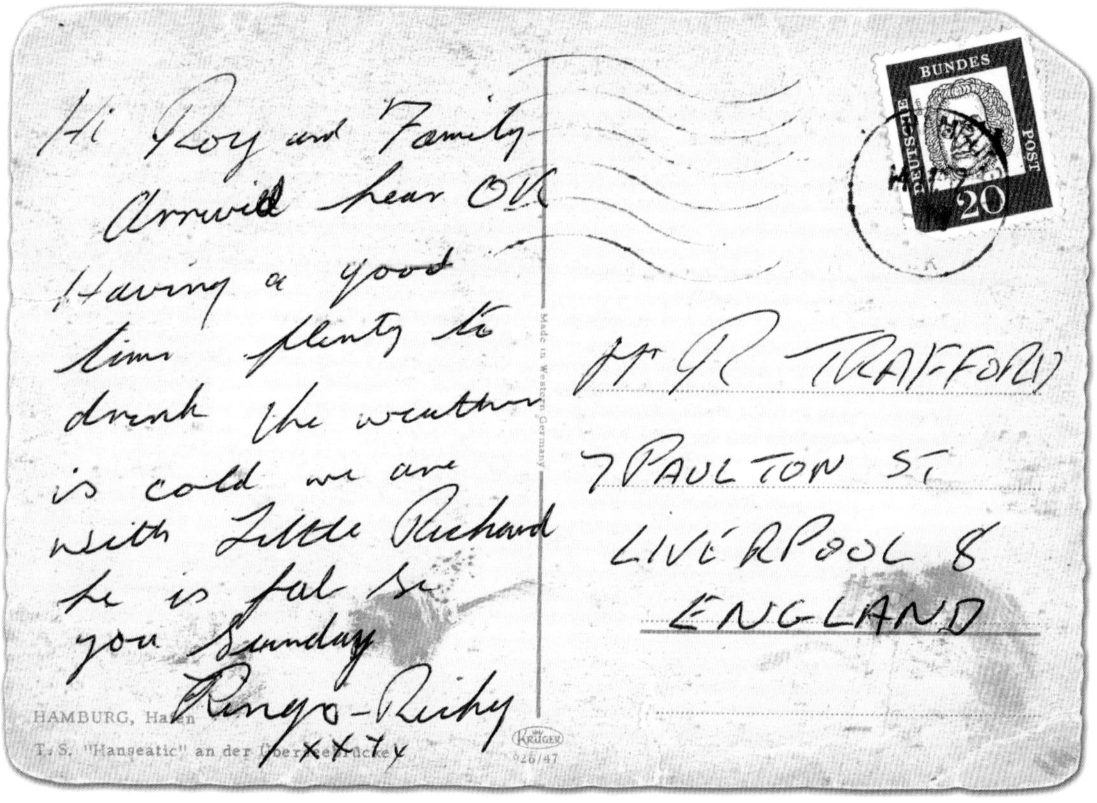

Hi Roy and Family
Arrived hear OK
Having a good
time plenty to
drink the weather
is cold we are
with Little Richard
he is fab se
you Sunday
Ringo-Richy
xxxx
DEUTSCHE BUNDES POST
20
Made in Western Germany
Mr R TRAFFORD
7 PAULTON ST
LIVERPOOL 8
ENGLAND
HAMBURG, Hafen
T. S. "Hanseatic" an der Überseebrücke
KRÜGER
926/47

Mersey Beat magazine

Read all about it for 3d

In 1961 Liverpool art student Bill Harry had the idea to launch a new magazine to cover and promote the city's growing rock 'n' roll scene. And while the word 'beat' was a seldom used musical term, it did have a meaning in relation to the area covered by a local policeman and consequently Harry was inspired to call his new magazine *Mersey Beat*.

The first issue was published on July 5, 1961 with a print run of 5,000 and among the customers was Brian Epstein, manager of the local NEMS music store. And as a local band called the Beatles, who were mentioned in the first edition and appeared on the cover of issue number two – under the front page headline 'Beatles Sign Recording Contract' – it's highly likely that Epstein's attention was drawn towards the group he would later manage via the pages of *Mersey Beat* and the story about recording with Mike Sheridan in Germany.

In fact Epstein contributed to *Mersey Beat* as a record reviewer and also regularly placed adverts for his NEMS store in the magazine while Harry, who went to college with Lennon, got his former class mate to contribute stories, poems and drawings to the magazine while other members of the Beatles dropped into the magazine's offices in Renshaw Street to answer the phone and even help out with the typing.

Many of Lennon's works in *Mersey Beat* often appeared under the heading 'Beatcomber' – "I used to write a thing called Beatcomber because I admired the column Beachcomber in the *Daily Express*" explained Lennon – and the young Beatle also paid to place a selection of five advertisements in the paper on the understanding that they were placed randomly throughout the pages.

They read: "Hot Lips, missed you Friday, Red Nose; Red Nose, missed you Friday, Hot Lips; Accrington welcomes Hot Lips and Red Nose; Whistling Jock Lennon wishes to contact Hot Lips; Red Scunthorpe wishes to Jock Hot Accrington."

As more and more groups from Liverpool began to emerge, *Mersey Beat* organized a local music poll – which the Beatles topped for the first time in January 1962 (ahead of Gerry and the Pacemakers and the Remo Four) despite the band filling in the voting coupons themselves – and introduced charts and gig guides alongside release listings before expanding to cover cities such as Manchester, Birmingham and Newcastle. Harry also hired a young up-and-coming Liverpool singer called Priscilla White to write a fashion column and the story goes that when he couldn't remember her name – but he knew it was colour – he made it up. "The black bit came when a local paper called *Mersey Beat* had a misprint. They knew my surname was a colour and guessed wrong!" the chart-topping Cilla Black later confirmed.

In 1964 Harry was persuaded by Epstein to move to London and merge *Mersey Beat* into a new national music paper called *Music Echo* but when things didn't work out he resigned and went on to become the press agent for acts such as the Kinks, the Hollies, David Bowie, Led Zeppelin, Cockney Rebel and Kim Wilde before writing a host of Beatles-related books. Meanwhile, *Mersey Beat*, under the banner *Music Echo*, was eventually acquired by the owners of *Disc* magazine and merged to form a new title *Disc & Music Echo* – with no mention of *Mersey Beat*.

(Right) *Mersey Beat*'s music poll edition in 1962, featuring the Beatles' victory and an advert for manager Brian Epstein's NEMS music stores.

ERSEYSIDE'S OWN ENTERTAINMENTS PAPER

MERSEY BEAT

Vol. 1 No. 13   JANUARY 4-18, 1962   Price THREEPENCE

Beatles Top Poll!

FULL RESULTS INSIDE

Cover photograph by Albert Marrion

JOHN LENNON   GEORGE HARRISON   PAUL McCARTNEY   PETE BEST

IN THIS ISSUE

CLUBLAND

PERSONALITIES

JAZZ

FEATURES

ALSO

POLL RESULTS

1 JACK O' CLUBS
3 N.U.R. No. 5 SOCIAL CLUB
7 ODD SPOT OPENS

4 ALEX POWER
BERT DONN
TOM HARTLEY
JOHNNY SANDON

5 LEO RUTHERFORD
6 MERSEYSIDE JAZZ

EDITORIAL
8 NEMS TOP TEN

ARTISTES DIRECTORY
CLASSIFIED
ADVERTISEMENTS
MERSEY ROUNDABOUT

Beatles Fan Club membership card

Ten years and 80,000 members

Just a few months after *Mersey Beat Hot* was created to report on Liverpool's rapidly growing music scene, the Beatles earned their own devoted fan club when Bernard Boyle set up an unofficial appreciation society for the group which was capturing the headlines around Merseyside.

Created in September 1961, it existed into 1962 when an official fan club was created and run by Roberta Brown from her home win Wallasey. Eventually Cavern regular Freda Kelly – who took over from Brown – was given a job by manager Brian Epstein in his NEMS organization on the condition that he got control of the fan club. "Eppy said if we gave him the fan club subscription money, he'd pay the bills," was how she explained the arrangement.

As the Beatles became more famous and began to collect fans throughout the UK, it was proposed that a National Secretary, based in London, should be appointed and operate out of Epstein's London offices in Monmouth Street. While Kelly remained as Northern Secretary, Anne Collingham was named as head of the London office even though she didn't exist and was simply a name on the notepaper. However, there were at least five full-time (and real) workers employed to deal with the vast amount of mail which arrived from Beatle fans.

Signed-up members of the Beatles fan club received membership cards, newsletters and special offers including exclusive records and even fan club only shows at the Cavern. And 3,000 of them travelled to Wimbledon Palais on Saturday December 14, 1963 for the Southern Area Fan Club Convention were they got a chance to meet, collect autographs and even kiss each of fab four before watching a special 'fans only' live show.

By 1965 there were over 80,000 paid up Beatles fans but the club was still not a profitable operation and had to be continually supported financially by Epstein and his company when Kelly took over running the national operation from Liverpool. The Beatles official fan club finally closed in March 1972.

On the back of the Beatles' huge success in the early 1960s, a magazine called *The Beatles Book* or *Beatles Monthly* was launched by publisher Sean O'Mahoney in August 1963. He was given permission by Epstein and the group to launch his title which started with a run of 80,000 copies and had passed the 300,000 mark by the end of the year. While Beatles' roadies Neil Aspinall and Mal Evans wrote articles for the magazine, there was also an official fan club segment included in each edition and cartoons by Bob Gibson who later worked on drawings for the group's *Magical Mystery Tour* album.

After a total of 77 editions, *The Beatles Book* ceased publication in December 1969 although it was revived in 1976 when all the original issues were republished, but it finally closed in 2003.

(Right) Beatles Fan Club membership cards issued from the original Liverpool office and the later London address, where they were 'signed' by the fictitious Anne Collingham.

The Official
Beatles FAN CLUB
P.O. Box No. 12,
LIVERPOOL, 1.

THIS IS TO CERTIFY THAT

...... Judith Coulson......................

IS AN OFFICIALLY ENROLLED MEMBER
OF THE FAN CLUB AND HAS BECOME
BEATLE PERSON NUMBER

118587.

Freda Kelly
National Secretary of The Official Beatles Fan Club

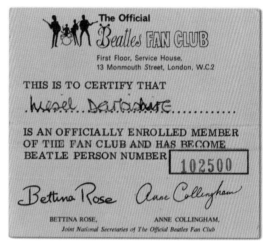

The Official
Beatles FAN CLUB
First Floor, Service House,
13 Monmouth Street, London, W.C.2

THIS IS TO CERTIFY THAT

Wesel Darbishire..............

IS AN OFFICIALLY ENROLLED MEMBER
OF THE FAN CLUB AND HAS BECOME
BEATLE PERSON NUMBER

102500

Bettina Rose   Anne Collingham

BETTINA ROSE,   ANNE COLLINGHAM,
Joint National Secretaries of The Official Beatles Fan Club

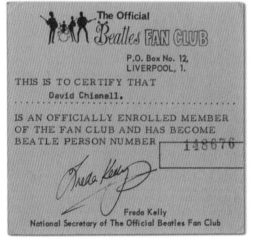

The Official
Beatles FAN CLUB
P.O. Box No. 12,
LIVERPOOL, 1.

THIS IS TO CERTIFY THAT

David Chisnell.
....

IS AN OFFICIALLY ENROLLED MEMBER
OF THE FAN CLUB AND HAS BECOME
BEATLE PERSON NUMBER   148676

Freda Kelly
National Secretary of The Official Beatles Fan Club

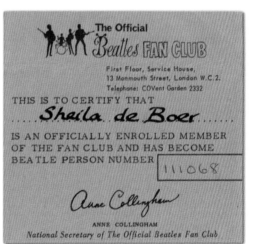

The Official
Beatles FAN CLUB
First Floor, Service House,
13 Monmouth Street, London W.C.2.
Telephone: COVent Garden 2332

THIS IS TO CERTIFY THAT

..... Sheila de Boer.......

IS AN OFFICIALLY ENROLLED MEMBER
OF THE FAN CLUB AND HAS BECOME
BEATLE PERSON NUMBER   111068

Anne Collingham

ANNE COLLINGHAM
National Secretary of The Official Beatles Fan Club

Tower Ballroom poster

Into the big time

Possibly the biggest gig the Beatles had played in their short time together came on November 10, 1961 when they were booked to appear at the massive 5,000 capacity Tower Ballroom in New Brighton. Although they didn't fill it, over 3,000 people packed into the ballroom to see a show that was termed *Operation Big Beat* and featured a number of Liverpool groups.

Put on by local promoter Sam Leach, the show saw the Beatles appear at 8pm and then again at 11.30pm and in between they dashed off to nearby Knotty Ash to play a show in the village hall. They were back two weeks later for *Operation Big Beat II* when they topped a bill which included Rory Storm and the Hurricanes, Gerry and the Pacemakers and the San Remo Four while hit-maker Emile Ford was a surprise guest, jumping on stage to appear with the Hurricanes. Tickets cost 6/- (30p), there were three licensed bars and the show ran through until 2am.

The Tower Ballroom was located on the Wirral Peninsula in the seaside town of New Brighton which is part of Merseyside's Wallasey district. When it was erected in 1900, the Tower was the tallest iron construction in Europe and the ballroom continued to thrive even after the Tower was pulled down in 1921.

The Beatles third show at the Tower Ballroom was on December 8 and followed a lunchtime show at the Cavern. At both venues they backed singer Davy Jones while South African singer Danny Williams was a late edition to the bill and on December 15 they returned again to play alongside Cass and the Casanovas.

In 1962 the Beatles topped the Tower Ballroom bill on January 12 – when Screaming Lord Sutch failed to turn up for what was advertised by Leach as 'The Greatest Show On Merseyside' – and between January and April they made a further five appearances. The next time they played at the Tower Ballroom – on June 21, 1962 – they were booked by their manager Brian Epstein and

he opted to put them on as second on the bill to the hit-making American singer Bruce Chanel.

Now advertised as 'Parlophone Recording Artistes', the Beatles returned to headline Leach's *Operation Big Beat III* on June 19 before supporting Joe Brown and his Bruvvers on Epstein's *NEMS Enterprises* show on June 27. By the time the Beatles returned to the Tower Ballroom three weeks later, drummer Pete Best had been sacked and replaced temporarily by the Big Three's Johnny Hutchinson.

Operation Big Beat V and a special show to celebrate Rory Storm's birthday marked the Beatles' two September shows at the Tower before Epstein put them on the bill on October 12, 1962 with rock 'n' roll star Little Richard who was paid £500 to appear. "Brian started to promote shows himself so he could put on his own bands," recalled roadie Neil Aspinall. "He'd hire the Tower Ballroom and get a star like Little Richard who was touring England. But the Beatles would always be second on the bill to the big visiting star."

On November 23 the Beatles raced back from a BBC TV audition in London to appear at the 12th annual Lancashire and Cheshire Arts Ball when they joined Billy Kramer and the Dakotas on the Tower bill and they made a December 1 appearance as last-minute additions to a seven-act bill.

On June 14, 1963 the Beatles returned to the Tower Ballroom after six months away to appear as headliners on a *Mersey Beat Showcase* presented by NEMS and manager Epstein who had slowly edged out Leach, the man who originally booked them to play at the Tower Ballroom which was destroyed by fire in 1969.

(Right) A 1962 poster shows the Beatles as top of a bill featuring rival Liverpool bands. These included Billy Kramer, before he added a 'J' and changed the name of his backing group to 'the Dakotas'.

LEACH ENTERTAINMENTS PRESENT

OPERATION BiG BEAT - 5TH

AT THE

TOWER BALLROOM NEW BRIGHTON
FRI. 14TH SEPT. 7·30 - 1·0 A.M.

FEATURING AN ALL STAR 6 GROUP LINE UP · STARRING
THE NORTH'S TOP ROCK COMBO. APPEARING AT 10·30 PROMPT

The BEATLES

RORY STORM WITH THE Hurricanes

GERRY AND THE PACEMAKERS | THE 4 JAYS

BILLY KRAMER WITH THE COASTERS | THE MERSEY BEATS

TICKETS 5/-

* **LICENSED BARS** (UNTIL 12·15 A.M.)

* LATE TRANSPORT (ALL AREAS L'POOL & WIRRAL)
COACHES LEAVE ST. JOHN'S LANE / LIME ST. 7·00 - 8·30 P.M.
FROM
RUSHWORTHS · NEMS · CRANES · STROTHERS
LEWIS'S · TOP HAT RECORD BAR · TOWER BALLROOM

Neil Aspinall's business card
From classmate to company boss

Welsh-born Neil Aspinall returned to Liverpool with his mother during World War II and eventually went to the Liverpool Institute where he first met classmate Paul McCartney and George Harrison who was in the year below.

"Behind the air-raid shelters at school there used to be this smoking club; that's where I first met Neil", recalled Harrison, while Aspinall recounted that he was making his way to McCartney's house when he first met John Lennon in Liverpool's Penny Lane. Employed as an accountant, Aspinall lodged with the Best family where he became involved with the Beatles as they were booked to play at the Casbah Club which was owned by Mona Best.

As their bookings in and around Liverpool began to increase, the Beatles went in search of someone who could drive and also had some sort of vehicle in which they put their instruments and Aspinall, with his grey and maroon Commer van, fitted the bill. After driving them around in 1961 – and charging them 5/- (25p) per person per gig – Aspinall gave up accountancy the following year to become the Beatles' first ever official road manager. John Lennon later confirmed, "Neil's our personal manager. He was in from the start – he went to school with Paul and George."

In 1963 Aspinall, together with fellow road manager Mal Evans, followed the Beatles to London – "we were the last ones to get a flat because we couldn't afford it" – and continued to work closely with the Beatles and gradually he became the group's personal assistant. In 1967 the Beatles formed the company Beatles & Co, which would later become Apple Corps, and following the death of manager Brian Epstein, Aspinall eventually became the company's managing director. "Neil did eventually take over and he became manager of Apple", recalls George Martin, "but at that time he wasn't of sufficient clout ... it was a very difficult time."

Ultimately Aspinall, who survived the arrival of Allen Klein as head of Apple, took on the mantle of loyal and discreet caretaker of all things Beatles' related as the four group members went their separate ways but remained linked through the offices and affairs of Apple. He represented the company in lawsuits against Klein, EMI and Apple Computers and, while ill-health restricted his involvement during the 1990s, he oversaw the creation and release of the Beatles' Anthology film, record and book projects. Sadly the man who drove the van, looked after all four Beatles and even played the harmonica on 'For The Benefit Of Mr Kite' and percussion on 'Magical Mystery Tour' died in 2008.

(Right) Beatles' road manager Neil Aspinall's business card – with a hand-written track listing – from the offices in Liverpool to which NEMS moved in August 1963.

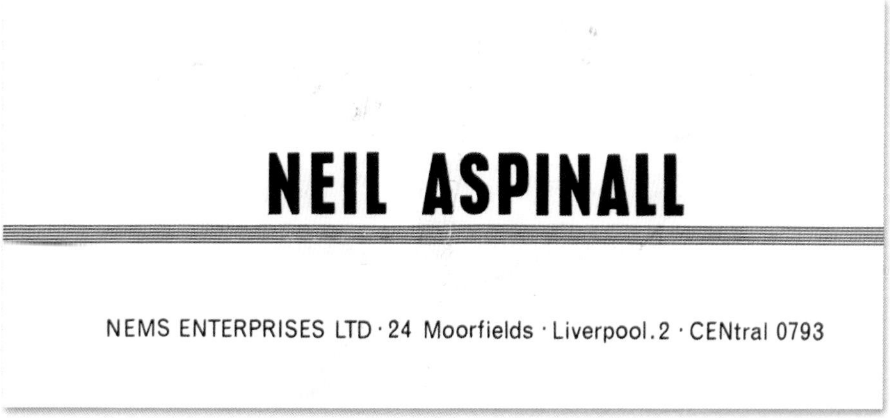

NEIL ASPINALL

NEMS ENTERPRISES LTD · 24 Moorfields · Liverpool. 2 · CENtral 0793

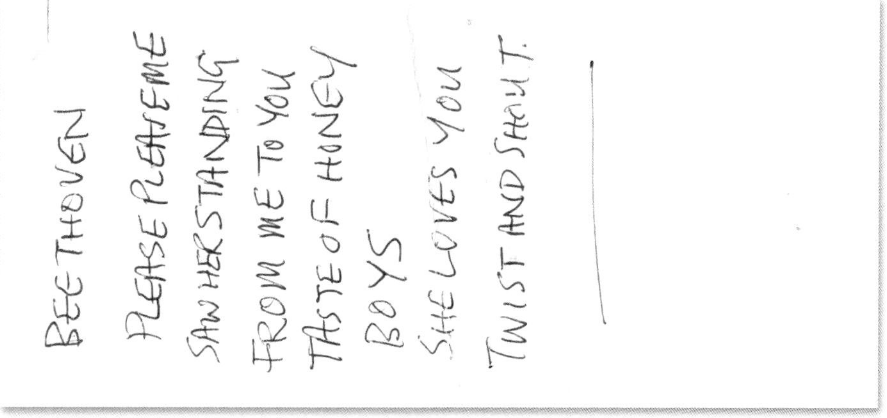

BEETHOVEN

PLEASE PLEASE ME

SAW HER STANDING

FROM ME TO YOU

TASTE OF HONEY

BOYS

SHE LOVES YOU

TWIST AND SHOUT.

(Right) Neil Aspinall (left) 'on duty' with the Beatles in 1964, as they make their way to the television studios in Teddington to film *Thank Your Lucky Stars*.

The Decca audition tape

"Groups are out"

The Beatles – Lennon, McCartney, Harrison and Best – spent New Year's eve 1961 trekking down to London in a van driven by the long-time roadie Neil Aspinall for an audition in front of a newly formed production team at the UK's second largest major record company Decca.

Manager Brian Epstein – who travelled down separately from Liverpool by train – had gone through a host of meetings with the company's executives including A&R chief Dick Rowe and producer Mike Smith before landing a test recording session in Decca's studios in Broadhurst Gardens in the north London district of Hampstead.

After a night spent in the Royal Hotel in Russell Square, the Beatles arrived at 11am on New Year's Day for their audition and nervously ran through 15 songs from their live shows including the Lennon & McCartney numbers 'Like Dreamers Do', 'Love Of The Loved' and 'Hello Little Girl', alongside their versions of American classics such as 'Searchin'', 'Til There Was You', 'Money', 'September In The Rain', 'Memphis' and 'Crying Waiting Hoping'.

By 2pm the audition was completed and Epstein and the group went for a meal before the Beatles and Aspinall drove back to Liverpool. While Smith gave Epstein some encouragement, he explained that the final decision was down to Rowe and the well-documented outcome was that Rowe, Smith and Decca opted for another band they tested on the same day, Brian Poole and the Tremeloes. Epstein alleged that Rowe had told him, "We don't like your boys' sound. Groups are out: four piece groups with guitars particularly are finished."

While Epstein left Decca without a contract, he was allowed to keep a copy of the audition tape and told he could use it in his efforts to get the Beatles a record deal. However in the 1970s and 1980s bootleg versions of tracks from the audition began to leak on to the market although they were never officially released by Decca.

In 2012 what was a described as the original safety master tape from the January 1, 1962 audition came on to the market. The demo, containing ten tracks on a 12 inch audio tape, was thought to have been in the possession of Epstein until he gave it to an executive with EMI who in 2002 sold it to a collector of music memorabilia. On December 2012, at an auction in London, a Japanese collector paid £35,000 for the tape.

(Right) The ten-track 'safety master tape' from the Beatles January 1962 audition for Decca Records, which was sold at auction in 2012.

TIME	TITLE
	TONES N.R.OUT 1k, 10k, 70Hz, DOLBY TONE 2 TRACK MON
	— SIDE 1 —
2:29	LIKE DREAMERS DO BSR-1111-A
2:17	MONEY
2:19	TAKE GOOD CARE OF MY BABY
2:17	THREE COOL CATS
1:57	SURE TO FALL 11:39=7
	— SIDE 2 —
1:46	LOVE OF THE LOVED BSR-1111-B
2:14	MEMPHIS
1:59	CRYIN' WAITIN' HOPIN'G
2:50	TIL THERE WAS YOU
2:57	SEARCHIN'

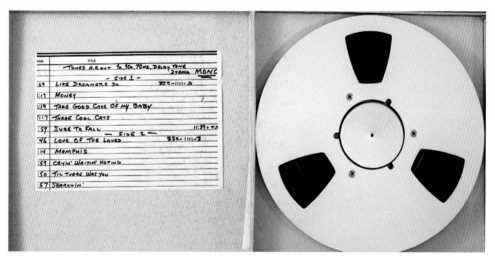

Beatles' boots

Stepping out in style

On the back of the Beatles' new clothes there also came an important change of footwear, with the group discovering Chelsea boots made by a London firm of shoe makers called Anello & Davide. They created footwear for the entertainment industry – ranging from shoes and boots for actors and singers to specialist shoes for ballet and tap dancers.

Founded in 1922, Anello & Davide supplied Marilyn Monroe, Pete Ustinov, Orson Welles, Jane Fonda and David Niven with shoes in addition to providing footwear for the cast of shows such as *Cats* and *Mama Mia* plus Judy Garland in the film *The Wizard Of Oz*.

Although it's lost in the mists of time which member of the Beatles or their 'inner circle' actually saw the tight-fitting ankle length boots with pointed toes in the window of a Covent Garden shoemaker for the first time, the group's long-time confidant and eventual head of Apple Corps, Aspinall has a memory from early 1962. Following the group's audition for Decca Records on New Year's Day, he recalls that "We went down Shaftesbury Avenue and around there, and found amazing things to buy. The boot shop Anello & Davide was on one corner."

Harrison also recalled the same visit to London on January 1, 1962, and his first encounter with the new footwear. "The first pair of those boots I ever saw was on that trip. They had elastic in the edges and I found out that they were made in a shop in Charing Cross Road called Anello & Davide."

There are also references to Lennon and McCartney actually buying a pair of Chelsea boots in the same shop – when they went through London on their way back from a trip to Paris – and taking them back to Liverpool to show Harrison and Best, who promptly ordered a pair each.

Either way the Beatles – followed by such stars as Roy Orbison and Marc Bolan – eventually commissioned from Anello & Davide four pairs of Chelsea boots with raised Cuban heels. This modified version has gone down in history as 'a Beatle boot' and today a pair in calf leather can be bought for around £125.

(Right) Anello & Davide's black leather boots with a zip and Cuban heel.

(Far right) Paul McCartney, George Harrison and John Lennon sporting the 'Beatle boot' that they discovered in London in 1962 and made famous around the world.

Lennon's German work visa

Germany ... again

Following their stints at the Indra, Kaiserkeller and Top Ten clubs in Hamburg, the Beatles were happy to consider returning to Germany in 1962. By now Brian Epstein had appeared on the scene as the group's prospective manager and he quickly became involved in negotiations with Tom Ten Club owner Peter Eckhorn.

The German entrepreneur travelled to Liverpool in late 1961 to book acts for the following year and when he approached the Beatles, he was introduced to Epstein who was on the verge of signing a management deal with the group. Eckhorn at first offered to pay around 200DM per week to each group member but Epstein wanted 500DM each per week but he finally agreed to consider a deal of 450DM per week.

However, standing on the sidelines was a new club owner named Manfred Weissleder and he sent his manager to Liverpool in an effort to secure the Beatles for his yet to be named or opened rock venue. In January 1962 a contract was finally signed between Epstein and Weissleder which saw each of the Beatles being paid 500DM a week in return for a seven-week booking from April 13, 1962.

By the time the Beatles flew into Hamburg, the new club – in the city's notorious St Pauli district close to the Reeperbahn – was up and running as the Star Club but on their arrival the group were told that former band member Sutcliffe had died of a brain haemorrhage. However they fulfilled their string of shows which involved them playing four hours one night followed by three hours the next. And, according to Paul McCartney, what went on in Germany's major port city became a important part of the Beatles story. "Hamburg was certainly a great childhood memory. But I think all things are enhanced by time. It was very exciting, though I think it felt better to me a little later in our career, once we'd started to get a bit of success with the records."

Following their opening stint at the Star Club, John Lennon had to go through the process of getting a new visa that would allow him "to enter – to travel through – Germany". Giving his home address in Menlove Avenue and the address of Brian Epstein's NEMS store in Whitechapel, Lennon applied on August 30, 1962 in order to be able to return to join his band mates for two more visits to West Germany.

(Right) The Beatles backstage at the Star Club in 1962, with U.S. rocker Gene Vincent [right].

(Far right) John Lennon's application form for a visa, which allowed him to return to Germany in November and December 1962 for the Beatles' final shows at the Star Club.

Antrag

auf Erteilung eines Sichtvermerks zur Einreise nach — zur Durchreise durch — Deutschland

Application for a Visa to enter — to travel through — Germany

Demande de délivrance d'un visa d'entrée en — de transit par — l'Allemagne

An d__ Botschaft — Gesandtschaft — **Generalkonsulat der Bundesrepublik Deutschland**

To the Embassy — Legation — Consulate-General of the Federal Republic of Germany

Ambassade — Légation — Consulat Général de la République fédérale d'Allemagne

in / in / à

1. Familien- und **Vornamen** (bei Frauen auch Geburtsname)	**Lennon**
1. Surname and Christian names (in the case of married women state also maiden name)	(Familienname) (Surname) (Nom de famille)
1. Nom de famille et prénoms pour les femmes, nom de jeune fille)	**John Winston** (Vornamen, Rufname unterstreichen) (Christian names, underline name by which usually known) (prénoms, souligner le prénom usuel)
2. Geburtstag und Geburtsort (Kreis, Land)	geboren am Born on **9.10.40** né le
2. Date and place of birth (county, country)	in in **Liverpool, England** à
2. Date et lieu de naissance (département, pays)	(Kreis (county (département ... Land) country) pays)
3. Wohnsitz oder dauernder Aufenthaltsort, Sitz der gewerblichen Niederlassung, genaue Anschrift und Geschäftsadresse	**251, Menlove Avenue, Woolton, Liverpool 25.**
3. Domicile or permanent residence, and seat of business establishment, exact private and business address	**12-14, Whitechapel, Liverpool 1**
3. Domicile ou lieu de résidence permanente, siège de l'entreprise, adresse exacte privée et commerciale	**Entry Visa**
4. Familienstand	ledig Single **Single** célibataire
4. Marital Status	
4. Situation de famille	verheiratet, verwitwet, geschieden seit _____ Married, widowed, divorced since _____ marié, veuf, divorcé depuis _____
5. Staatsangehörigkeit (bei Doppelstaatern auch die weitere)	jetzige Present nationality **British** actuelle
5. Nationality (in case of dual nationality state second nationality)	frühere Former nationality _____ d'origine
5. Nationalité (en cas de double nationalité, indiquer aussi la seconde)	zweite Staatsangehörigkeit Second nationality _____ seconde nationalité
6. Beruf	
6. Trade or profession	**Musician.**
6. Profession **30th August 1962**	

Kons. 11
20000 11. 61 Gebr. Molinger.Baus.Bonn

Star Club signed menu

Hamburg for the last time

In November 1962 the Beatles returned to Hamburg to play the Star Club for a second time and this time their fee was upped to 660DM per man per week. They arrived with their new drummer in tow. Ringo Starr had been hired in August to replace Pete Best and the veteran of German shows as a member of Rory Storm's Hurricanes played 14 nights with his new group until November 14.

Finally, in December 1962, the Beatles returned to Hamburg for what would be their last round of German club dates. They opened – for an increased fee of 750DM per man each week – on December 18 and played 13 nights (they had Christmas Day off) until December 31, which was also when former member of the Big Three Adrian Barber finished his unofficial recording of the Beatles performing at the club. The tapes were subsequently released in 1977 under the title *The Beatles Live! At The Star Club In Hamburg Germany 1962* and the album made it to number 111 in the US charts.

At the time Paul McCartney saw the trips to Germany as a possible chance to put some cash aside for a rainy day. "In Hamburg we used to think, 'we'll have to save money here in case it all finishes'," he said while George Harrison saw the adventures in Europe as lucrative affairs for the places they played in. "Hamburg was really happening then and they were coining quite a bit of money in those clubs; with all the drinks and the admission fees. They'd have four shows so they could get four different audiences in a night."

However by the end of their final engagement in Hamburg's Star Club – despite it being the plushest rock venue they had performed in, where the customers were able to order food and drink at their tables – the Beatles had had enough of the demanding work load. "We outlived the Hamburg stage and wanted to pack that up", said John Lennon. "We hated going back to Hamburg those two last times."

In June 1964 the original Star Club closed its doors and, after several unsuccessful attempts to revive it, the building at 39, Grosse Freiheit was destroyed by fire in the 1980s.

And after playing for a total of 279 nights in four Hamburg clubs between August 1960 and December 1962, the Beatles also moved on. As George Harrison remarked, "I'd have to say with hindsight that Hamburg bordered on the best of Beatles times."

(Right) Signed by all four Beatles, this Star Club menu card offered Coca-Cola for 1.20DM and a double measure of Rum-Grog for 3DM, plus a 10 per cent service charge.

(Overleaf) Looking out directly into the spotlights, George Harrison and John Lennon face their massed audience at Hamburg's Star Club in 1962.

Star-Club

Rock n' Twist-Parade 1962

Hamburg-St. Pauli, Große Freiheit 39

Getränkeauswahl

Drinks / Grand choix de boissons Stor sortering i drycker

Flasche Bier	0,33 l	1,50	Eierlikör	2 cl	1,50
Glas Wein		1,50	Curacao	2 cl	1,50
Rum-Grog	4 cl	3,00	Cherry Brandy	2 cl	1,50
Steinhäger	2 cl	1,50	Pfefferminzlikör	2 cl	1,50
Doornkaat	2 cl	1,50	Cacao mit Nuß	2 cl	1,50
Aquavit	2 cl	1,50	Apricot Brandy	2 cl	1,50
Gin	2 cl	1,50	Triple Sec	2 cl	1,50
Jamaika Rum, original	2 cl	1,50	Eier-Likör	2 cl	1,50
Reiner Weinbrand	2 cl	1,50	Cordial-Medoc	2 cl	1,50
Flensburger Dokator	2 cl	1,50	Masagen-Kaffee	2 cl	1,50
Underberg	2 cl	1,50	Bärenfang	2 cl	1,50
Wodka	2 cl	1,50	Jägermeister	2 cl	1,50
Whisky nach Wahl	2 cl	2,50	Mampe Halb und Halb	2 cl	1,50
Orig. Franz. Cognac	2 cl	2,50	Cointreau, orig. franz.	2 cl	2,50
Orig. Pernod Fils	2 cl	2,50	Chartreuse, orig. franz.	2 cl	2,50

dazu Soda . . . . DM 0,50

Coca-Cola	1,20	Zitronenlimonade	1,20
Fanta	1,20		

Preise zuzüglich 10 % Personalzuschlag.

Extra charge for staff 10 %.

Supplement pour personnel 10 %.

Till priserna räknas 10 % Personalavgift.

Das Personal ist angewiesen, Rechnung zu erteilen, auf den Pfennig abzurechnen und berechtigt, sofort zu kassieren.

Waiters are instructed to submit accounts, they must not round off amounts and they are authorized to collect accounts immediately.

Le personnel est tenu de remettre une note en rendant compte par addition jusqu'au pfennig, et est autorisée à demander un règlement immédiat.

Personalen är anvisad att lämna en nota och räkna mycket noga samt berättigad att genast inkassera beloppet.

Flaschenware umseitig.   For bottled beverages see reverse side.

Tarif des boissons en bouteilles au verso.   Drycker i flaskor se omstaende sida.

Parlophone promo card, signed
A label for life

After being turned down by the UK's two biggest record companies – EMI and Decca – the Beatles were in a position where they had been refused an opening by half of the major companies who dominated British pop music in the early 1960s. With only Pye and Phillips left to them, it was fortunate that manager Brian Epstein was offered a second chance by the largest music company – EMI – thanks to the man who ran their 'third' label, Parlophone.

The notable post-Beatles success of the label was in stark contrast to its beginnings in Germany before World War I, when record manufacturer Carl Lindstrom set up Parlophone as a home to classical recordings. In 1927, the British-based Columbia Graphophone company purchased Lindstrom's operations including Parlophone, which back then bore a German letter 'L' as its logo, and it was from this that the famous £ logo developed.

The formation of EMI in 1931, following the merger of the Gramophone Company with the Columbia business, brought Parlophone into the new British major and while it was home to US stars such as Nat Gonella and Duke Ellington, the label also released recordings by such stars as Leslie Hutchinson and Victor Sylvester. However, these British acts opted to leave the label during World War II when Richard Tauber – an Austrian Jew who had fled Germany in 1938 – was the only major act on the label which became known as 'Tauberphone'.

Guildhall School of Music graduate George Martin was hired by the label in 1950 in an effort to develop the roster of UK acts and he was involved in a string of hit records by such stars as Dick James, Eamonn Andrews, Charlie Drake and Johnny Dankworth. By 1962 Martin was running Parlophone, which operated in the shadow of the Columbia and HMV labels. They boasted Ruby Murray, Russ Conway, Cliff Richard, the Shadows and Helen Shapiro alongside Alma Cogan, Johnny Kidd and the Pirate, John Leyton and Danny Williams, among others.

Described by Martin as "on the sidelines, a bit like the Liberal Party", Parlophone boasted a handful of hit acts such as Scotland's Jimmy Shand, Germany's Obernkirchen Children's Choir, trumpeter Humphrey Lyttelton, skiffle group the Vipers, comedian Pete Sellars, pianist Mrs Mills, rock singer Adam Faith and the Temperance Seven.

These successes, which were described at the time by EMI chairman Sir Joseph Lockwood as "a few odd bits each year", finally led to Martin offering the Beatles a contract in June 1962 to record for Parlophone for one year and be paid 1d (one old penny worth 0.41 new pence) per double-sided single sold. The agreement also gave Parlophone three one-year options on the Beatles, while the 1d royalty was to be split between the four group members and their manager Brian Epstein.

It seems that the deal came about after Epstein, tired of waiting for a call back from the record company, had threatened to withdraw EMI's HMV, Parlophone and Columbia product from his NEMS shop while Martin acknowledged, "To say I was talking a gamble would be stretching it because the deal I offered them was pretty awful."

However, on the back of the success of their early Parlophone releases, the Beatles were offered an improved contract in June 1963. This earned them a royalty of 2d per record – at a time when a single cost 6s 7½d (33p) – and also brought such stars as Cilla Black, Billy J Kramer, the Fourmost and the Hollies to the label.

By 1969 the Beatles had released a record-breaking 17 UK number one singles ... all on Parlophone.

(Right) A signed Parlophone promotional card with details from a 1962 Beatles' set list. They dropped both 'Rhythm and Blues' ('A Shot of Rhythm and Blues') and 'Fool Of Somebody' ('If You Gotta Make a Fool of Somebody') from their shows in 1963.

THE BEATLES

lots of love
ON
PARLOPHONE
LORRAINE
from
THE BEATLES
RECORDS

George
Harrison
XXX

Ringo Starr

John Lennon

Paul McCartney
XXXXX

SAW HER STANDING THERE.
RHYTHM & BLUES.
DO YOU WANNA KNOW A SECRET.
BEAUTIFUL DREAMER.
ANNA.
THANK YOU GIRL
FOOL OF SOMEBODY.
SWEET LITTLE 16.
FROM ME TO YOU.

LONG TALL SALLY.

Ringo's Abbey Road ashtray

Sold for £135

One of the 'must-have' items in Abbey Road's studio two during any Beatles session was the ashtray on a stand which had a regular place alongside Ringo Starr's drum kit as he played on the band's recordings.

Smoking in the studios was still a regular habit in the 1960s and as all four Beatles were smokers, ashtrays were an integral piece of equipment during their sessions, but Starr's chosen receptacle actually dated back to the earliest days of the studio.

Abbey Road was opened on November 12, 1931, just less than six months after the formation of EMI in the summer of 1931 and had originally been built as a nine-bedroomed house in 1830 on a site in the prestigious north London suburb of St John's Wood. It continued to be used as a private residence until local builder Francis Myers, who bought the property in 1929 for £12,000, sold it to the Gramophone Company for £16,500.

Then, in the summer of 1962, a quartet from Liverpool joined producer George Martin in the studio. "It was fantastic to be in Abbey Road", said Paul McCartney who added that he was "pretty nervous on most occasions in the recording studio".

Although the ash tray – which measures around 75cm (2'6") high – became known as 'Ringo's ashtray', it had been used by drummers and pianists from the 1930s onwards with popular pianist Mrs Mills often having it placed alongside her piano in the studio. In fact when she went into hospital during the 1960s, she asked for the ashtray to be sent to her bedside and she returned it to the studio when she left hospital.

With the introduction of a no-smoking rule in the studios in the late 1970s, the ashtray was relegated to a storeroom until it was brought out to be sold as part of an auction of studio equipment held at Abbey Road in October 1980. It was bought for £135 but the lady who purchased it contacted studio manager Ken Townsend, who had also bid for it, a few years later and offered to sell it back to him for the same price.

A copy of Brian Epstein's book *A Cellarful Of Noise* – signed by the Beatles and producer George Martin – was also sold that day (for £210) alongside a Mellotron used on *Sgt Pepper's Lonely Hearts Club* album, which was bought by musician Mike Oldfield for £1,000, and a roll of toilet paper with 'EMI' stamped on every sheet which had been given to Townsend by the Beatles as a present when he was promoted to technical manager. "I had a call to go to studio two to see the Beatles as they had a serious complaint to make about the studios", recalls Townsend. "The group were stood behind the mixing desk and John Lennon held the roll of toilet paper which he said was 'too hard and too shiny' and, because it had EMI printed on it, it meant we didn't trust our staff. He gave me the roll and because I didn't realize it was a wind-up I went and spoke to the studio manager and that afternoon we changed all the toilet rolls in Abbey Road to softer paper."

The roll of toilet paper appeared on BBC TV's *Antique Roadshow* in September 11 when it was brought along by the son of the man who had bought it in the auction for £85.

As a result of the days the Beatles spent at Abbey Road, both the studio and the pedestrian crossing have become a popular haunt for visitors who have gathered on the crossing to reproduce the famous cover shot from the final album, sprayed graffiti on the walls and even stolen the Abbey Road road signs off the wall. In 2010 the studio building was granted a Grade II English Heritage listing and in the same year the pedestrian crossing was also given Listed Building status.

(Right) Ringo's Starr's famous ashtray, which was used regularly for over five decades in Abbey Road studios by drummers and pianists before being auctioned off.

Ticket for Hulme Hall

A new drummer arrives

Port Sunlight has a number of claims to fame including its origins as a model village built for workers at the Lever Brothers soap factory and as the place where Ringo Starr made his first ever professional appearance with the Beatles.

Hulme Hall was a small venue in Port Sunlight with a capacity of just 450 and it was a regular venue for dances and parties which attracted local groups who would travel across the River Mersey from Liverpool. On July 7, 1962 the Beatles – with drummer Pete Best – were booked to appear at a local golf club dance but by the time they returned on August 18 for the local Horticultural Club's show dance, Best had been fired and Starr was in the drummer's seat.

Before joining the Beatles, Starr had spent time as drummer with the Darktown Skiffle Group and Al Caldwell's Texans who eventually became Rory Storm

and the Hurricanes. Regulars on the Liverpool circuit, including shows at the Cavern, the Hurricanes also topped the bill in Hamburg, where Starr eventually joined Tony Sheridan's backing band. However, he eventually returned to the Hurricanes and it was during their summer season booking at Butlin's holiday camp in Skegness that he was approached by John Lennon and Paul McCartney who offered him £25 a week to join the Beatles.

The posters for his debut appearance with them – which ran from 7.45pm until 11.30pm with tickets costing 6/- (30p) – announced that the dance would be "starring the North's No. 1 rock combo, the Fabulous Beatles, now recording with Parlophone." The Beatles' contract required them to play for a minimum of an hour and for no more than 80 minutes and they were paid a group fee of £30.

(Left) The Beatles recording their first ever radio interview for local hospital radio at Hulme Hall in October 1962.

(Right) A ticket from the After Show Dance held in Hulme Hall on Saturday August 18, 1962, when Ringo Starr made his debut with the Beatles, just three days after Pete Best had been sacked.

THE PORT SUNLIGHT HORTICULTURAL SOCIETY

After Show Dance

will be held in

HULME HALL, Port Sunlight

on

SATURDAY, 18th AUGUST, 1962

THE FABULOUS BEATLES BAND
SUPPORTED BY THE 4 JAYS

SPOT PRIZES

Dancing 7.45 p.m. to 11.30 p.m.

BUFFET

Tickets 6/-

TAXIS—Phone Rock Ferry 1135 or 3077

Beatles harmonica

Produced but never sold

It seems that the first instrument any of the Beatles ever learned was the mouth organ which John Lennon began playing as a school boy in Liverpool. He recalled that his Auntie Mimi used to take in students and one of them had a mouth organ and seemingly made a deal with the young Lennon. "[He] said he'd buy me one if I could learn a tune by the next morning. So I learnt two. I was somewhere between eight and twelve at the time, in short pants anyway." He also recalled travelling to visit his aunt in Edinburgh and taking his new instrument with him. "I played the mouth organ all the way on the bus ... things like Swedish Rhapsody, Moulin Rouge and Greensleeves."

It seems that the driver of the bus to Scotland was so impressed by the young Lennon's ability that he gave him a better mouth organ – "he gave me a fantastic one – it really got me going", recalled Lennon. Years later, in his earliest collaborations with Paul McCartney, Lennon used the harmonica when writing songs and occasionally during their early live shows, but it was when they came to record their first single for Parlophone in September 1962 that the instrument came to the fore.

In fact Lennon hoped that by using the harmonica on 'Love Me Do', he would give the humble mouth organ its big break as a pop instrument but he was beaten to it when it appeared on Frank Ifield's chart topping single 'I Remember You' in July 1962. During the session in Abbey Road on September 4, 1962, Lennon played a Hohner Marine Band harmonica which he also used on later recordings of 'Please Please Me' and 'I Should Have Known Better' and he later recalled, "'Love Me Do' is rock 'n' roll, pretty funky; the gimmick was the harmonica."

Hohner, who began making musical instruments in Germany in 1857, manufactured accordions, kazoos, flutes, banjos and ukuleles but specialized in harmonicas and at one time made over a million a year. The ten-hole, 20-reed Marine Band harmonica was a favourite model with professional musicians and Lennon was particularly impressed by the solo played by Delbert McClinton on Bruce Channel's March 1962 hit Hey Baby. In fact when the Beatles played on the same bill as Channel in June 1962, Lennon spent time getting tips from the American player.

While Paul McCartney once remarked that Lennon's harmonica part on the Beatles' first ever hit single was "a great bit" and added that "John was a good harmonica player", Lennon remembered a conversation he had with the Rolling Stones harmonica player Brian Jones in which he explained that he used a harmonica with a button on 'Love Me Do' "because you couldn't get 'Hey Baby!' licks on a blues harp."

In 1964, on the eve of the band's first tour of America, Hohner struck a deal with the Beatles' manager Brian Epstein for the sale of the Beatles' harmonica at a price of $2.98. In their advertising Hohner suggested, "It is anticipated that the Beatles identification will make their harmonica package a best seller, as the mop-headed entertainers have done with other products using their name. Hohner expects to keep the merchandise in adequate supply."

And all was well and good except for the fact that on the packaging, which featured a picture of each Beatle alongside their autograph, the German company's art department had put McCartney's photo together with Harrison's signature. As a result the product was never actually released.

Nearly 50 years after Lennon's mouth organ solo appeared on the first Beatles' first hit record, Hohner, in conjunction with Yoko Ono, launched the John Lennon Signature Harmonica, featuring a cartoon self-portrait of Lennon plus his signature. The white harmonica came on to the market in April 2012 at a price of $99.

(Right) A $2.98 Beatles harmonica made by Hohner, who made the mistake of putting Paul McCartney's and George Harrison's autographs under the wrong photographs on the box.

'Love Me Do' signed single

Making a personal appearance

The first record released by the Beatles under their recording contract with EMI's Parlophone label was a song written by Lennon and McCartney when they were both teenagers in Liverpool. This also featured as one of the first songs written by the group to be included in their live act.

'Love Me Do' was in fact recorded on three separate days during 1962 in EMI's Abbey Road studios in the north London district of St John's Wood. On June 6 Lennon, McCartney, Harrison and Best recorded it during a session beginning at 6pm under the direction of producers George Martin and Ron Richards, plus engineer Norman Smith. The group recorded four songs – 'Besame Mucho' plus three Lennon-McCartney songs 'Love Me Do', 'P.S. I Love You' and 'Ask Me Why' – while Martin retired to the canteen for a cup of tea.

After he had been called back to takeover the session, Martin gave instructions for a standard recording contract to be drawn up and, oddly, backdated it to June 4, 1962. By the time the Beatles returned on September 4, Best had been replaced by Ringo Starr but the focus during this 7pm to 10pm session was on the song that would become the group's first single release.

A song written by Mitch Murray called 'How Do You Do It' was recorded alongside 'Love Me Do' and it was Martin who ultimately decided. "I looked very hard at 'How Do You Do It' but in the end I went with 'Love Me Do'. It was quite a good record." Martin was unhappy with one aspect of the recording and he decided to change things for the final September 11 session.

"George [Martin] didn't like Ringo," recalled McCartney. "Ringo at that time was not that steady on time. To George he was not as pinpoint as a session guy would be." As a result Martin brought in top session drummer Andy White and his job during the 10am until 1pm session was to drum on 'P.S. I Love You' while Starr played the maracas. On the next take of 'Love Me Do', White was

again on drums – with Starr this time on tambourine.

While 'Love Me Do' was chosen as the first official release by the Beatles, when it came out on October 5, 1962 as Parlophone 45-R 4949 there was still confusion as to who was playing drums on which version. Copies pressed before 1963 featured Starr on drums from the September 4 session while copies after that had White on drums from the September 11 session. It seems that the change was brought about by the release of the EP *The Beatles' Hits* in September 1963 which featured White on drums and the decision that all future pressings of 'Love Me Do' would feature this later version.

When the single was released, there was another spot of confusion as McCartney's name on the record's composer credits was spelt McArtney on the initial run of promo copies for radio and music papers although it was corrected for the first commercial pressings.

The Beatles first official recording was released into the market place with adverts in *Record Retailer* and *Mersey Beat* and to help things along locally Epstein chose not his own NEMS store but Dawsons Music Shop in Widnes in Cheshire - 15 miles across the Mersey from Liverpool – as the venue for his group's first ever personal appearance and record signing on the day after the release.

Booked to play at Hulme Hall in the evening, the Beatles arrived at 4pm and stayed for an hour during which time each member of the group signed copies of their red label Parlophone single – the version with Ringo Starr on drums that is pictured right.

'Love Me Do' peaked at number 17 in the charts amid rumours of manager Epstein buying as many as 10,000 copies of the record to help it up the charts and went on to become the group's fourth US number one in May 1964.

(Right) During an in-store record-signing session in Cheshire, the Beatles autographed early copies of their debut single 'Love Me Do' on the red Parlophone label.

Ardmore & Beechwood contract
Getting a shilling in advance

Back in the early days of pop music – as radio and television began to play an important role in the development of both hit records and artists – it was song publishers who did the bulk of the work when it came to getting records played.

Having worked on selling songs as sheet music before discs became common place, the publishers found songs, bought the rights to them and then spent both time and money promoting them. So when two members of Brian Epstein's new group the Beatles began to emerge as composers, the manager was forced to consider getting a publishing deal alongside a recording contract.

With the Beatles signed to EMI's Parlophone label and their first record set for release in October 1962, Epstein – who later admitted "I really had no idea what publishing meant" – opted to take the easy route and sign Lennon and McCartney's first two songs with a company linked to EMI.

Ardmore & Beechwood had been established in the UK in 1958 as small subsidiary of EMI's American Beechwood Music business and was run out offices above the EMI-owned HMV shop in Oxford Street. Syd Coleman was the company's general manager and when Epstein went into the HMV shop on May 8, 1962 to transfer his tapes on to a record, the engineer sent a message to Coleman suggesting that he meet with Epstein to discuss a possible publishing deal.

While Coleman was impressed with the original Lennon and McCartney songs, Epstein was more interested in getting a recording deal for his group and it was only after they had signed to Parlophone that he turned his attention to a deal to cover the first two titles 'Love Me Do' and 'P. S. I Love You'. Signing to EMI for both recording and publishing was a common-sense move and the publishing deal offered by Ardmore & Beechwood was arguably no more generous than the recording deal which offered the Beatles a royalty of 1d per double sided single – split between the four group members and Epstein.

The agreement with Ardmore & Beechwood was signed on September 7 1962 by Epstein on behalf and Lennon and McCartney and it brought the composers an advance of 1/- (5p) against royalties in return for full copyright 'for all countries'. Under the terms of the deal the composers received a 10% royalty after the first 500 sales of sheet music in the UK; 50% royalty from all record sale in the UK; 50% of all fees received from the Performing Right Society (PRS) and 50% in overseas royalties from the songs being published in 'foreign territories'.

In their role as music publishers, Ardmore & Beechwood were expected to get the first Beatles recording played on the radio and also arrange television appearances for the group, but the performance of both the publishers and the record company was a disappointment. The managing director of EMI Records, L G Wood, said the record "didn't do well" and described sales of 17,000 as "not all that good".

And despite the group's debut single reaching number 17 in the chart, Epstein was even more disappointed in the performance of the music publishers as he told the Beatles producer George Martin. "Brian was furious with Ardmore & Beechwood over their poor performance with 'Love Me Do' and decided not to give them any more Lennon/McCartney songs."

Bizarrely 'Love Me Do' and 'P.S. I Love you' are the only two songs written by Lennon and McCartney which are owned by McCartney who negotiated ownership of them from Capitol Records – which owned the Ardmore & Beechwood catalogue – as part of the deal which saw him re-sign to Capitol Records, from CBS Records, in the mid-1980s.

(Right) The first publishing contract for songs written by John Lennon and Paul McCartney, which was negotiated and signed by Brian Epstein in September 1962.

An Agreement

made this **7th** day of **September** 19 62

BETWEEN BRIAN EPSTEIN for and on behalf of "LENNON/McCARTNEY" of

(hereinafter referred to as " the Composer ") of the one part and Ardmore & Beechwood Limited

363, Oxford Street, London, W.1.

in the County of London (hereinafter referred to as " the Publishers ") of the other part

WHEREBY IT IS AGREED as follows :—

1. In consideration of the sum of £ **1/-d** on account of the royalties hereinafter made payable paid to the Composer by the Publishers (the receipt of which sum of £ is hereby acknowledged) the Composer hereby assigns to the Publishers THE FULL COPYRIGHT FOR ALL COUNTRIES in the musical composition ENTITLED

LOVE ME DO and P.S. I LOVE YOU

Including the title, words and music thereof in all Countries for the period of copyright as far as it is assignable by law, together with all rights therein which he now has or may hereafter become entitled to whether now or hereafter known and any renewals thereof, where the initial copyright subsists in a specific Country the laws of which provide for such renewals of copyright, including the publishing rights, the performing rights, the synchronisation rights, the television rights the right to use the same for mechanical reproduction and the right to make, publish, perform and reproduce any arrangement, alteration or adaptation of the same.

2. The Composer hereby warrants that the said composition is an original work and that he is the owner of the copyright therein and that he has not granted, transferred or assigned any interest in the copyright hereby assigned or any part thereof to any person and that the said composition has not been published with his consent or acquiescence.

3. The Publishers will pay to the Composer the following royalties subject as hereinafter provided :

   (a)   **10%** upon each complete copy of the said composition over and above the first 500 copies sold by the Publishers in the United Kingdom of Great Britain and Northern Ireland and

   (b)   **50%** of royalties received from gramophone records, excluding medley records (less cost of collection) for sale to and use by the general public in the United Kingdom of Great Britain and Northern Ireland

   (c)   **50%** of all royalties received from persons authorised to publish the said composition in foreign territories.

   (d)   **50% of all fees received from the Performing Right Society Ltd., until such time as the writers become members of that Society.**

4. The Publishers shall be under no obligation to pay any other sums whatsoever except as in this agreement provided, and no royalties shall be paid upon the following: complimentary copies of the said composition, copies sold but not paid for, copies sold and returned to the Publishers, copies given away as new issues or for advertising purposes, copies published in selections, albums, newspapers, magazines and other periodicals.

5. The Publishers will render to the Composer statements showing the monies derived from the use of said composition for which payment is to be made to the Composer as provided in this agreement, for each six months period ending 30th June and 31st December in each year, within ninety (90) days after each of said dates.

6. The Composer hereby undertakes to indemnify the Publishers against all claims, damages and demands and against all costs and expenses incurred in the institution or defence of any action or proceeding relating to the right, title and interest of the Publishers in and to the said composition.

7. The Composer hereby agrees that he will not transfer or assign the benefit of this Agreement or any part thereof without the written consent of the Publishers first had and obtained

8. It is also understood and agreed that the Publishers shall have the right to transfer and assign any and all rights under this agreement, providing all the terms of this Agreement are observed.

9. The Publishers shall have the right to make and publish new adaptations and arrangements of said composition and to make such additions and adaptations and alterations in and to the words and/or music of said composition that it may desire, and to provide and translate the lyric thereof in any and all languages of the licensed territory.

10. The Composer will upon the Publishers request at any time execute for the Publishers any assignments or any other documentary evidence or papers in connection with the establishing and maintaining of the Publishers said ownership and rights in the said composition.

11. That were sheet music, records, publicity etc. is concerned credit will be given to Lennon/McCartney

In Witness whereof the Composer and Publishers have set their hands the day and year first before written.

McCARTNEY/LENNON

COMPOSER   ARDMORE & BEECHWOOD LIMITED.

Vox AC30
Amplifying the sound of the Beatles

Just after the Beatles made their recording debut at EMI's Abbey Road studios in June 1962, the group's manager went off in search of a deal for new equipment which the group could use.

In July Brian Epstein made his way to Jennings Musical Industries store in London's Charing Cross Road in an effort to arrange a deal for a set of Vox AC30 amplifiers. Jennings manufactured and distributed the Vox amps which were made in the company's factory in Dartford, Kent. As a result of their ever-expanding date sheet, the group's equipment was in need of an update and Epstein's idea was for Vox to donate a set of amps to the Beatles who, he explained to the people at Jennings, "Were going to be big and do so much promotion (for Vox) that it would pay off a thousand times over."

The deal saw Jennings take the Beatles' old amps as a trade-in for a pair of AC30s in a Vox tan colour which would have cost around £100 each. The engineers at Vox produced an add-on treble boost unit for the Beatles' amps and over the years continued to expand the capabilities of the AC30, which rapidly became the 'must-have' equipment for the new groups that were part of Britain's emerging beat boom.

The Beatles first used their new tan-coloured AC30s on July 27 at a show in the Tower Ballroom, New Brighton, which was promoted by Epstein and featured Joe Brown as the headline act. Even though Epstein had promised that his group would happily appear in any Vox promotional efforts and material, they did not make it on to Vox's 1962 list of top 20 acts, which was headed by the Shadows, but by 1963 they began appearing in newspaper adverts for Vox's 'Precision Sound Equipment'.

During their six-night residency at Margate's Winter Garden in July 1963, the Beatles made a visit to Vox's Dartford factory and John Lennon and George Harrison took possession of a pair of new black AC30s which came with new carrying handles, while Paul McCartney acquired a new AC30 bass amp. A Vox executive later commented, "We gave them whatever they wanted, no questions asked."

By July 1964 the Beatles had moved on from their AC30 amp and were using new Vox AC50 amps, costing around £250 each, while McCartney had an AC100 bass amp. By the time they reached America in August, they had upgraded to AC100 guitar amps. During this first US tour, rival equipment manufacturers began hustling Epstein for a share of the Beatles' equipment business, with Fender leading the way while Vox took trade adverts which carried "a message to the American Music Trade" and pronounced, "You are being invaded by a series of British performing groups who feature VOX equipment, the forerunners of whom were the Beatles."

(Above) A Vox amp, which the Beatles used for more than five years in the studio on stage.

(Right) Under Brian Epstein's deal with Vox amps, the Beatles were regularly featured in the company's adverts.

(Right) Standing between two Vox amps, George Harrison tunes his guitar during a July 1963 recording session at Abbey Road studios.

'Please Please Me'

The single

In the days before there were official British Phonographic Industry (BPI) awards for record sales, the gongs were handed out by the music paper *Disc*, which focused on the pop music of the day and competed directly with *Record Mirror* for the attention of the nation's younger readers.

Launched in 1958, *Disc* (later to become *Disc & Music Echo*) introduced sales awards in 1959, taking sales figures from the record companies and presenting silver discs for 250,000 sales and gold discs for sales of over one million. In 1963 the Beatles received their first ever sales award in the shape of a disc: a silver disc for a quarter of a million sales of their second single 'Please Please Me'.

The group's follow up to 'Love Me Do' was recorded in Abbey Road, under the direction of producer George Martin, on November 26, 1962 in a session running from 7pm to 10pm. While the records and credits show 'Please Please Me' as a joint composition by John Lennon and Paul McCartney – albeit credited to McCartney/Lennon on the album sleeve – the song was primarily written by Lennon. And while McCartney admitted "Please Please Me was more John than me", Lennon made his claim to the song clear in a note sent to *Melody Maker* in 1971.

To accompany the release of 'Please Please Me' on January 11, 1963, the Beatles' manager Brian Epstein recruited independent PR man Tony Calder (later to launch Immediate Records with Andrew Loog Oldham) to issue a press release which proclaimed that "THE BEATLES have made THE RECORD OF THE YEAR" and predicting that the single would "put this exceptional vocal/instrumental quartet high up on the NATIONAL TOP TEN CHARTS within the next fee weeks."

While producer Martin, who has asked the Beatles to "change the tempo" and speed it up, told the group on the day they recorded the song that "you've just made your first number one" and *New Musical Express*

(*NME*) declared that it was a "really enjoyable platter, full of beat, vigour and vitality – and what's more, it's different"; the argument still goes on as to whether 'Please Please Me' was in fact the group's first chart topper.

While it topped the record charts in *NME*, *Melody Maker* and *Disc*, it only reached number two – behind Frank Ifield's' 'The Wayward Wind' – in the music industry publication *Record Retailer* which in January 1963 had begun publishing a new independently audited Top 50 which then became accepted as the 'official' music business chart.

Whether 'Please Please Me' went to number one or not the Beatles were awarded the silver disc, which was presented to them on April 5, 1963 by Martin in the offices of EMI in Manchester Square, London.

And so busy were the Beatles in the spring of 1963 that after they had visited EMI House – and given a private live performance for the company's executives – they made their way to the Swimming Baths in Leyton High Road in East London for another show.

(Left) The advert taken out by Parlophone in 1963, when the Beatles topped the *New Musical Express* chart with 'Please Please Me'.

(Right) Years later John Lennon sent this card to *Melody Maker* – following an interview with George Martin by writer Richard Williams – explaining that he wrote 'Please Please Me' "alone".

Dear George Martin / Richard Williams
            _I_ wrote **Please** **Please**
me _alone_. it was recorded in
(the exact ◯ Sequence
in which i wrote it.
        "Remember?"
            love John & Yoko
⊙〇---
L.P. WINNER.

Melody Maker
161 Fleet S
London
EC4P 4AA.

TO SEE
THROUGH
UNO
71

Thank Your Lucky Stars invitation

On national telly

After the relative failure of the Beatles' debut single 'Love Me Do', manager Epstein was adamant that he wanted to move the group's song publishing away from Ardmore & Beechwood and one of the people he was recommended to see was the aspiring music publisher Dick James.

James was a big band singer whose biggest solo chart success came with 'Robin Hood', the theme song to the popular 1950s TV series, which was produced by George Martin and released on Parlophone Records in 1956 when it rose to number four in the charts. And it was Martin who suggested that Epstein should meet James, who had formed Dick James Music in September 1961, to discuss a deal involving the songs written by Lennon and McCartney.

James' son Stephen is prepared to admit that his father's publishing business was in trouble at that time – "He hadn't had any great success and he was actually running out of money" – so his meeting with Epstein in late 1962 in his offices at 132, Charing Cross Road in London's Soho district was a welcome opportunity.

Epstein arrived for the meeting with an acetate of the Beatles' new single 'Please Please Me' and told James that if he worked the single and made it a hit, his company could have the music publishing rights to the songs written by Lennon and McCartney. With that, James rang his friend Philip Jones, who was producer of the important TV pop show *Thank Your Lucky Stars*, and played the record down the phone to him. He was rewarded with an immediate booking for the Beatles on the show which shown nationally on a Saturday night.

Thank Your Lucky Stars was made by the Birmingham-based independent TV network ABCTV and was launched on the ITV network in April 1961 with Pete Murray as host and Anne Shelton and the Dallas Boys as the main attractions. On January 14, 1963 the Beatles travelled to ABC's studios in Aston, Birmingham to pre-record their performance of 'Please Please Me' before going on to play a sold show in Ellesmere Port, Cheshire at the Wolverton Welfare Association Dance. Their debut on national TV came five days later when *Thank Your Lucky Stars* was broadcast on January 19, with the Beatles featured at the bottom of a seven act bill.

The Beatles went on to make a further nine appearances on *Thank Your Lucky Stars*, with the show broadcast on April 3, 1965 marking their final performance in the studio. Alongside *Ready Steady Go*, which was launched in August 1963, *Thank Your Lucky Stars* was at the heart of the UK television's pop music shows, but the independent franchise system, which saw new companies take over local broadcasting rights, brought about the demise of the show in 1966.

The Beatles, whose first opportunity to appear on television throughout the UK came on *Thank Your Lucky Stars*, were also featured in the last ever show, on June 25.

(Above) An invitation to watch *Thank Your Lucky Stars*.

(Right) The Beatles on stage at the Television Studios in Teddington on July 1, 1964, recording 'A Hard Day's Night' during their appearance on *Thank Your Lucky Stars*.

Northern Songs letter

Getting into music publishing

Having met up with music publisher Dick James – and in return for him getting the Beatles on national TV – Brian Epstein kept his promise and decided that he was the right man to handle the music publishing interests of Lennon and McCartney after the poor performance of Ardmore & Beechwood.

Before he set about creating a new official partnership, Epstein showed his gratitude to James, whose company Dick James Music included accountant Charles Silver as a partner and an aspiring young musician named George Martin as one of its composers, by handing over the publishing rights to 'Please Please Me' and its B-side 'Ask Me Why' to James in exchange for an advance of one shilling and a royalty of 10% to the composers.

In February 1963 – four months after he was given Please Please Me – James formed Northern Songs in partnership between his own company, writers Lennon and McCartney and Epstein's NEMS operation. While the company was split to give James 50% with the other 50% shared between NEMS and the two writers, it seems that James and Silver retained one more voting share giving them a 51% advantage.

James wrote to the Performing Rights Society on March 14, 1963 to tell them about the creation of the new company and also to transfer the copyright in five Lennon and McCartney songs – 'Misery', 'I Saw Her Standing There', 'There's a Place', 'Hold Me Tight' and 'Do You Want To Know a Secret' – from his company into the new Northern Songs business.

Over the years, as Lennon and McCartney became more aware of how the music business worked – and music publishing in particular – they became more disappointed in the deal their manager had done with Dick James. "I think Dick James might have carved Brian up a bit", said Lennon while McCartney reflected on his earnings from the most covered song of all time. "Brian did some lousy deals and he put us into long-term slave contracts. For 'Yesterday', which I wrote totally on my own, I am on 15%. To this day I am only on 15% because of the deals Brian made."

In an effort to avoid the punitive levels of income tax which existed in the mid sixties – the top rate stood at 83% plus a further 15% surtax for high earner – the Beatles were advised to turn Northern Songs into a public company and sell shares to the public. On February 15, 1965, one and quarter million shares of the company's five million 2/- (10p) shares were put on sale with the remaining 3,750,000 shares being split between James and Silver (937,500 each), Lennon and McCartney (750,000 each) and NEMS (375,00), with Harrison and Starr each buying 40,000 shares each.

Valued on the Stock Exchange at £2.7 million, Lennon and McCartney each took £94,270 in cash which, in the absence of Capital Gains Tax (which came into effect in April 1965) was tax free income. Following the death of Epstein in 1967, James eventually decided to sell his shares in Northern Songs and opted to go with his old agent Sir Lew Grade and his ATV company despite interest from the Beatles. His decision once again prompted a bitter response from McCartney who reflected on the sale of Northern Songs. "So it was sold and it became merchandise then. It was bought by Lew Grade. So that was how John and I lost ownership of so many of our songs."

After a second bidding war in the early 1980s, ATV Music – including Northern Songs and over 250 songs composed by Lennon and McCartney – was bought by Michael Jackson for $47.5 million. Today, the most famous and valuable catalogue of popular songs is with Sony Music, following their merger with ATV Music in 1995.

(Right) The letter which music publisher Dick James wrote announcing the formation of Northern Songs in 1963, with five songs written by John Lennon and Paul McCartney.

DICK JAMES MUSIC LIMITED

SUITE TWO, 132 CHARING CROSS ROAD, LONDON, W.C.2

TELEPHONE
TEMPLE BAR 1687/8.

CABLES
DEJAMUS, LONDON-WC2

DIRECTO
RICHARD L.JAMES

DJ/RD

14th March, 1963.

R. J. H. Neil Esq.,
The Performing Right Society Ltd.,
Copyright House,
29-33 Berners Street,
London, W. 1.

P. R. S. LTD.
(S)
Recd. 15 MAR 1963
Ansd.

My Dear Dick,

Re: NORTHERN SONGS LIMITED

This is to inform you of the incorporation of a music publishing
company with the above name.

I will furnish you with all the information you require at the
earliest possible moment. Perhaps you will be good enough to let me
know all the details you will need.

It will be necessary to assign several copyrights from Dick James
Music Limited to Northern Songs Limited the first of which will be:

MISERY	(John Lennon and Paul McCartney)				
I SAW HER STANDING THERE	"	"	"	"	"
THERE'S A PLACE	"	"	"	"	"
HOLD ME TIGHT	"	"	"	"	"
DO YOU WANT TO KNOW A SECRET	"	"	"	"	"

Beatles' bug logo

A beetle for a Beatle

As the Beatles prepared for their first major UK tour in February 1963 – with teenager singing star Helen Shapiro as top of the bill – it was decided that the time had come to further emphasize the group's name and smarten up their stage presence.

When he joined the Beatles in 1962, Ringo Starr had brought with him the Premier drum kit he had used with Rory Storm and the Hurricanes which had his name emblazoned across the front of the bass drum. In an effort to ensure that nobody thought the band were called the Ringo Starr Band and in an effort press home the name the Beatles to the fans, it was decided that a group logo was needed for the front of the drum kit.

First of all Paul McCartney took on the task and came up with some 'roughs' based around the idea of using a 'bug' as a logo. These sketches were passed on to Liverpool sign writer and artist Tex O'Hara, whose brother was known to the Beatles as he was a member of the Fourmost, who were also managed by Epstein. He came up with a selection of drawings and, when the group chose their favourite, it was printed on to a piece of linen, stretched across the front of the drum and held in place on the rim by mounting clips. The script style word 'Beatles' was then adorned with beetle antennae on the capital B of Beatles.

While nobody is certain as to when the new 'beetle' logo was actually created, delivered or first used by the Beatles, it seems that the drum with Starr's name on it was still in use in January 1963 but had been replaced with the new logo by the time the group went into Abbey Road studios to record their debut album. The 'beetle' design was also on show when they performed on ATV's *Thank Your Lucky Stars* in February and it went with them to their most bizarre booking – at Stowe public school on April 4 1963 when a Liverpool-born student at the school wrote directly to Epstein asking if the group would appear.

And even though it seems that the beetle-style Beatles' logo was a short-lived device, it was used by the EMI's French record company Odeon in an advertisement for records in the programme that went with the Beatles' appearances at the Olympia Theatre in Paris in January and February 1964.

However in the UK, by the time the group travelled to Birmingham to appear on *Thank Your Lucky Stars* on May 12, 1963 – performing 'From Me To You' for transmission on May 18 – they had a new band logo printed on Starr's bass drum. And this one featured the iconic drop T and enlarged capital B in the name Beatles – a design that was to stay with them through to their last ever live shows in America in 1966.

(Above) The reverse of the first Beatles' album released in France, including a clipping from the *Financial Times*.

(Right) Designed in Liverpool in 1963, the Beatles 'beetle bug' logo was featured on the cover of the French version of the album *Please Please Me*, which was entitled *Les Beatles*.

Please Please Me album

All in a day's work

There are at least two extraordinary facts to note about the Beatles first album *Please Please Me*. Firstly that it was completed in only three recording sessions spanning just one day and secondly it carried the unique song writing credit of McCartney/Lennon on the eight tracks composed by the two group members.

On February 11, 1963, after an absence of over two months, the Beatles returned to Abbey Road to join producer George Martin and engineer Norman Smith in the studio. The previous evening they should have been on stage in Peterborough performing as part of their tour with Helen Shapiro, but in order to make the first 10am session they were excused duty.

When they arrived in the studio Martin was keen to know what songs they could record quickly and the answer was their stage act. According to Starr it was the obvious solution: "We knew the songs because that was the act we did all over the country. That was why we could easily go into the studio and record them."

Anxious to get an album out as soon after the success of the single 'Please Please Me', Martin was confident that the Beatles could record ten tracks during ten hours spread over three sessions – 10am until 1pm, 2.30 to 5.30pm and 7.30 until 10.45pm. With 'Love Me Do', 'P.S. I Love You', 'Please Please Me' and 'Ask Me Why' already in the can, the Beatles began with 'There's A Place' and 'Seventeen' (the working title of 'I Saw Her Standing There') in the morning session and added 'A Taste Of Honey', 'Do You Want To Know A Secret' and 'Misery' during the afternoon.

In the final evening session they worked through the unused 'Hold Me Tight', followed by their cover versions of the songs 'Anna', 'Boys', 'Chains' and 'Baby It's You' before, at around 10pm Lennon took the larynx-busting lead vocal on 'Twist And Shout'. "John sucked a couple more Zubes, had a bit of a gargle with milk and away we went," recalls Smith.

Producer Martin, who had kept 'Twist And Shout' until the very end, recounts, "We did two takes and after that John didn't have any voice left at all. It was good enough for the record and it needed that linen-ripping sound."

By August 1963, and the release of the Beatles' third single 'She Loves You', the song-writing credit used on their first album – and also on 'From Me To You' and the EP *Twist And Shout* – had been changed to the ever-familiar Lennon/McCartney. It seems that someone had the idea that Lennon/McCartney sounded better and despite McCartney famously quipping "not to me it doesn't", that was how it stayed. "I wanted it to be McCartney/Lennon", he added, "but John had the stronger personality and I think he fixed things with Brian."

While they were happy with the record, it seems that at least one of the group was less than happy with the cover photograph taken by Angus McBean over the balcony on the first floor of EMI's Manchester Square offices. "The *Please Please Me album* cover is crap," observed Harrison, "but at that time it hadn't mattered. We hadn't even thought it was lousy, probably because we were so pleased to be on a record."

"Crap" cover or not, the album *Please Please Me* was released on March 22, 1963 and entered the UK album chart on April 6, reaching number one on May 11 when it ended Cliff Richard's 14-week run with *Summer Holiday*. During its 30-week stay at the top, the album sold over 500,000 copies in the UK. With new locally designed cover artwork, it helped establish the group in France, where in January 1964 they played a 19-day residency at the prestigious Olympia Theatre, and in Germany where local language versions of 'I Want To Hold Your Hand' and 'She Loves You' became major hits.

(Right) An early German version of the *Please Please Me* album (top) and a later French album that was re-issued with an Apple logo.

Three US flops

"Forget it. They're nothin'"

When Capitol Records executive Dave Dexter, after listening to the Beatles' first recordings, told his colleagues "They're a bunch of long-haired kids. Forget it. They're nothin'", he created an opportunity for the group's manager to seek out alternative companies to release their records in America.

First on the horizon was Vee Jay, a Chicago label named after the first initials of founders Vivian Carter and Jimmy Bracken, which had signed a deal with EMI in the early 1960s, giving them the rights to release Frank Ifield's 'I Remember You' alongside access to the Beatles' recordings in the US, at a cost of $20,000 per record.

Their first release was the single 'Please Please Me' – with 'Ask Me Why' as the B-side – on February 25, just six weeks after its UK release. In addition to failing to achieve any sort of commercial success for the single, Vee Jay also managed to misspell the group's name on the label as 'The Beattles'.

Undaunted, Vee Jay opted to release 'From Me To You' – the Beatles' first official UK number one (it topped the charts in industry magazine *Record Retailer)* – on May 27, 1963, with 'Thank You Girl' on the flip side. While it appeared on local US radio station playlists, the single stalled at 116 on the national charts and it ended the relationship between Epstein and Vee Jay and prompted McCartney to note, "'From Me To You' was released – a flop in America. 'Please Please Me' released over there – flop."

In search of the elusive breakthrough in America, Epstein switched his attention to Swan Records, a small independent based in Philadelphia which boasted US disc jockey and TV host Dick Clark among its early investors. They issued 'She Loves You' on September 16, 1963 and a week later the US music magazine *Billboard* included it among a list of 'Four Star Singles' which they recommended to dealers. At the same time disc jockey Murray the K was playing the record on New York's WINS station, where listeners voted it into third place in a poll of five new singles.

Yet still the record failed to make any real impression and Ringo Starr once remarked, "We had three out on Vee Jay and Swan but nobody had them or had even heard of us." Finally, however, after Capitol decided to issue 'I Want To Hold Your Hand', the three earlier unsuccessful releases picked up sales. 'Please Please Me' eventually reached number three in the US in March 1964 – with 'From Me To You' as the B-side – and 'She Loves You' earned Swan Records their only US number one when it topped the charts on March 21, 1964.

(Above) The original US version of 'From Me To You', which was issued on Vee Jay in 1963 and failed to make the Top 100.

(Right) It was issued a second time by Vee Jay in 1964 when it came out as the B-side to 'Please Please Me'.

(Above and right) Swan records earned their first and only US number one with 'She Loves You' in 1964, while Vee Jay's release of 'Please Please Me' peaked at number three in the American chart in the same year.

'From Me To You' press release
Reading NME on the road

When the Beatles set off on tour with Helen Shapiro on February 2, 1963, they were still celebrating the success of their second single 'Please Please Me', and there were already demands for a new single.

"Brian Epstein and I", said George Martin, "worked out a plan in which we tried – not always successfully – to release a new Beatles single every three months and two albums a year." So after 'Love Me Do' in October 1962 and the follow up in January 1963, the next step was a third single in April – and they didn't disappoint.

With Martin urging them to "give me another hit", the Beatles took time out during the second half of the Shapiro tour – when they were bottom of a six act bill featuring Danny Williams and Kenny Lynch – to craft their next release. It was while travelling on the tour bus from York to Shrewsbury on February 28 that Lennon and McCartney put their heads together to create 'From Me To You'.

"We weren't taking ourselves seriously – just fooling about on the guitar", explained Lennon. "Before that journey was over we'd completed the lyric, everything. The first line was mine and we took it from there." When they came up with the title 'From Me To You', Lennon began to consider what might have inspired him and his song-writing partner.

He thought back to the copy of the *New Musical Express* he had read in order to check the group's chart placing and realized, "We'd got the inspiration from reading a copy on the coach. Paul and I had been talking about one of the letters in the From Us To You column." If, as seems likely, they had been looking at the February 22 edition of *NME* there were only two letters published that week – one from a reader asking why "peals of maniacal laughter seem to crop up on records" (and he cited 'Limbo Rock' and 'Limbo Baby' as examples) and another letter which suggested that Cliff Richard had overtaken Elvis in the battle for chart success.

Just five days after they wrote the song – "'From Me To You' was both of us, very much together" was McCartney's recollection of the track – the recording of the single was completed in seven takes during an afternoon session in Abbey Road studios along with the B-side 'Thank You Girl' and it was released – on schedule – on April 11 with the number R 5015.

'From Me To You' took the Beatles to new heights. It was their first undisputed number one, sold over 650,000 copies and held the top spot for seven weeks.

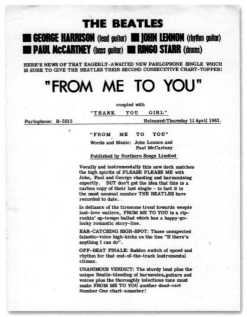

(Above) The official press release for the single 'From Me To You'.

(Right) Beatles' press clippings.

(Overleaf) Influential radio and television presenter Brian Matthew put his opinion of the Beatles and their single 'From Me To You' in writing for all to see.

BEATLES WAX NINE OF THEIR TITLES

THE Beatles' first LP—now called "Please Please Me"

BEATLES MAKE THE TOP

THE Beatles—who hit the No. 1 spot in MM's Pop 50 this week with "Please please me"—are set to join the Karl Denver Trio in a new BBC radio series, "Side by

The Beatles Challenge!

WOW! It's the Beatles all the way. Their second disc "Please Please Me" leaps to number three seriously challenging the Harris/Meehan top spot disc. And they go

...eries and tour for Beatles

THE BEATLES (page 12)
'Please' hits the top!

Week ending February 16, 1963

Last Week	This Week	Title	Artist	Label
2	1	Please, Please Me	The Beatles	Parlophone

BEATLES BOOKED FOR MAJOR TOUR

THE Beatles have been booked by promoter Arthur Howes for a nation-wide autumn tour with another Merseyside beat group, Gerry and the Pacemakers.

THE BEATLES
EXCLUSIVE!

You've PLEASED PLEASED us!

Page 4—MELODY MAKER. March 2, 1963

TOP FIFTY

1. (2) PLEASE PLEASE ME ...... Beatles, Parlophone
(3) THE WAYWARD WIND Frank Ifield, Columbia
THE NIGHT HAS A THOUSAND EYES
Bobby Vee, Liberty
Jet Harris and Tony Meehan, Decca
Frankie Vaughan, Philips
Springfields, Philips
Piccadilly

The Beatle...

...1963. MELODY MAKER—Page 3...

Beatles cut first LP

THE "Please please me" raced to No 2 in this week's MM Pop 50 — cut their first LP on Monday and have had their big seller released in the States...

Beatles, Pace... big new package

THE BEATLES, who this week win a Silver... "Please Please M... nationwide... Gerry and t... with their d...

Page 4—MELODY MAKER. March 9, 1963

TOP FIFTY

1. (1) PLEASE PLEASE ME ...... Beatles, Parlophone

a really z... It's...

...LATIONS ...ATLES CHARTS WITH ...EASE ME

what ...ch! ...ing Beatlewise

Group steals show

BRITAIN'S own Beatles stole the show when they joined forces with American stars Chris Montez and Tommy Roe at the start of a three-week tour last weekend. In fact, they closed the show for the second perform- ance last Saturday at East Ham.

...ys Chris Roberts

...received, Montez and ...have had very ...experience. With his fine ...and "Som... ...Montez... ...and...

pool that I spoke to guitarist- vocalist John Lennon, and bass guitarist-vocalist Paul McCartney.
"We don't play real rhythm blues," John began. ...not Ray Charles style ...though we used to do ...I say 'like everyone ...le of years ago. ...ical tastes are ...e a little bit of...

The BEATLES surround CHRIS MONTEZ (light jacket) an...

SCREAMS ACCLAIM BEATLES

NME TOP THIRTY

(Wednesday, February 27, 1963)

Last Week	This Week		
1	1	PLEASE PLEASE ME Beatles (Parlophone)	

...O HOFFMAN...

RINGO STARR

PAUL McCARTNEY

JOHN LENNON

GEORGE HARRISON

FROM BRIAN MATTHEW TO YOU—

A SPECIAL PRE-RELEASE QUOTE ON THE NEXT BEATLES SINGLE

"FROM ME TO YOU"

"I'll rate this no higher than another No.1!

If I could write songs half as good as FROM ME TO YOU I'd be laughing.

I'll put my shirt on it... and my suit...and my shoes...and, certainly, my best gramophone needle!!!"

"Visually and musically the most exciting and accomplished group to emerge since The Shadows"

— **BRIAN MATTHEW**

Beatles suits

A new straight image

After the Beatles had been persuaded to drop their leather look it was time for manager Brian Epstein to bring his influence to bear on the sort of outfits his new charges would wear on stage. By March 1962 he had them appearing onstage in suits which he bought from a local tailor based in Birkenhead.

Although outfitter Beno Dorn was across the River Mersey from Liverpool, he was well known throughout Merseyside and he regularly advertised in the local press with the slogan: "The master tailor for impeccable handmade clothes". Epstein took the Beatles "over the water" to Dorn's shop where he ordered four grey tweed suits with matching ties for £40 each which they wore for the first time on March 24, 1962 at a show for the Barnston Women's Institute in Heswell Jazz Club in Cheshire.

While wearing suits would ultimately lead to increased bookings and more money, Lennon was more opposed to the change than his three band mates. "So Brian put us in neat suits and Paul was right behind him. My little rebellion was to have my tie loose and the top button of my shirt undone but Paul'd come up to me and put it straight." While the suits represented a radical change for the Beatles – and Paul confirmed that it was a group decision when he said, "we all changed to the straight image" – they did see the value of the new smarter outfits. "Because we got mohair suits it was a bit like the black acts" was McCartney's take on the change which took them a shade closer to their new Motown heroes Smokey Robinson and Marvin Gaye.

Once in London, Epstein was obsessed with impressing record company, television and theatrical executives with 'his boys' and that meant more suits and time for a re-think on the wardrobe front. Epstein did his homework to ensure that his charges looked the part as Britain's newest top pop act and taking advice from established rock manager Larry Parnes (he looked after stars such as Billy Fury, Marty Wilde and Vince Eager) he visited show business tailor Dougie Millings in his Old Compton Street shop in London's Soho. There, the man who dressed Cliff Richard, Tommy Steele and Adam Faith got together with Epstein and the four group members to come up with a suit with a collarless jacket which was supposedly based on the uniform worn by ship's stewards.

Interestingly Lennon was once quoted as saying that during a trip to Paris in 1961, he saw French teenagers wearing flared trousers and round neck jackets. "So I went to a shop and bought one and thought 'oh we'll make suits out of this'. And they became Beatle suits."

Working from a design by French designer Pierre Cardin, Millings produced collarless dark blue and dark grey lightweight wool-and-mohair stage suits which the Beatles wore as early as the NME Poll Winners show in April 1963, on their autumn and winter UK dates and on their first US tour in April 1964.

Costing £31 per suit, Millings claimed he did "500 variations for the Beatles" – including four in each set, plus spares – and all in different shades. He also recalled that "there was always an extra one for John who got thin or fat or split his trousers running from the theatre".

Four original suits by Millings, who was dubbed "the Beatles' tailor", were provided to Madame Tussauds in London to be used on the first models of the 'fab four' which went on show in the famous wax works on April 29, 1964. The collarless 'Beatles' jacket' also became a must-have item for Beatles fans the world over who rushed out to buy copies, and even today a replica suit can be bought for £190.

(Right) Two of the outfits designed for the Beatles by London tailor Dougie Millings for shows in 1963 and 1964.

(Overleaf) The Beatles on the set of their film *A Hard Day's Night*, in bespoke suits by the tailor D.A. Millings & Son.

NME Poll winners programme

Four shows in four years

In the first half of the 1960s *New Musical Express* – or NME as it was known throughout the land – was the most popular pop paper easily outselling its rival *Melody Maker*, with its emphasis on jazz and pages of adverts for out of work musicians. It was also the pop paper which most enthusiastically got behind the Beatles when they emerged on the scene with their first major hit records in 1963.

Two of the paper's writers – Alan Smith and Chris Hutchins – had links with Liverpool through the newspaper *Mersey Beat* and they, with Brian Epstein, encouraged the paper to cover the Beatles' record releases, live appearances and growing influence of the pop music business. On February 1, 1963 Smith wrote about the success of the single 'Please Please Me' and suggested, "It looks like a bright future for the Beatles but knowing them I don't think they'll let it go to their heads" while Hutchins reviewed a show at the New Brighton Tower Ballroom on June 21 and concluded, "It was a fantastic night and one that echoed the success of these hit makers."

NME had initiated their Poll Winners concerts in 1953, a year after the paper's launch in March 1952, and by 1959 they were attracting stars such as Lonnie Donegan, Marty Wilde, Cliff Richard and Petula Clark to appear at their annual Pollwinners Concert.

In 1963 the Beatles made their first appearance at the *NME* Pollwinners' Concert, which was held at Wembley's Empire Pool on April 21. Appearing during the second half of the show – The Springfield, Frank Ifield, Adam Faith and Gerry & The Pacemakers featured in the first half – the Beatles were fifth on after Mike Berry, the Tornados, the Brook Brothers and Joe Brown and were followed by headliner Cliff Richard.

In fact the Beatles were last-minute additions to the 1963 show as they had not won any *NME* Awards by the time the concert was held but, on the back of the success of the singles 'Please Please Me' and 'From Me To You', they were squeezed in as the penultimate act to play their two hits, plus 'Twist And Shout' and 'Long Tall Sally' in front of their biggest audience ever. After the concert the Beatles bizarrely made their way into central London to play a supper club show at the fashionable Pigalle Club in Piccadilly.

Following their debut NME performance, the music paper suggested that "the Beatles look like being Poll Concert residents for many years to come". They were certainly regular Poll Winners between 1963 and 1970 collecting three awards for Single of the Year ('She Loves You', 'Eleanor Rigby' & 'Hey Jude'); Album of the Year for Let It Be; eight consecutive awards as UK Vocal Group (63–70); and seven awards as World Vocal Group (63–69).

(Above) Tickets for the NME Poll Winners Concerts.
(Right) A programme from the 1963 NME Poll Winners concert.

(Overleaf) American singer Tony Bennett (left) looks on as the Beatles receive an award at the 1965 NME Poll Winners Concert.

Presented by

THE 1962-63

ANNUAL

Poll-Winners'
All-Star Concert

EMPIRE POOL
WEMBLEY

Sunday, April 21st, 1963

Official Programme - - - Price 1/-

Concert handbill

Number one on the bill

In February 1963 the Beatles went on their first major UK tour with top of the bill Helen Shapiro plus singers Kenny Lynch and Danny Williams. It lasted a total of 14 nights – split into two parts – with the Beatles missing the last night of the first half on February 11 because they were recording.

The following month they embarked on a 21-date tour – running from London to Sheffield and Newcastle to Leicester – with American stars Chris Montez and Tommy Roe who shared top billing and were billed respectively as "America's exciting" and "America's fabulous". The Beatles were the top support act ahead of the Viscounts, the Terry Young Six and the 'glamorous'"Debby Lee and, despite the success of major UK acts such as Cliff Richard, Tommy Steel, Adam Faith and Billy Fury, still no British artist had ever topped the bill over a US star on a British package tour.

However that was to change when the Beatles went out on tour with Roy Orbison in May 1963. The tour opened at the Adelphi Cinema in Slough on May 18 and ran for a further 21 dates including shows in Glasgow and Cardiff. While Gerry and the Pacemakers were also on the bill, the official bill topper on the tour was Orbison although the Beatles actually closed the show.

Orbison later explained that when he arrived at a theatre he saw placards and posters of the Beatles. "There was very little of me", said the Texan singer who by that time had nine UK chart hits and was in the top ten with 'In Dreams'. "I asked them to take the placards down. I was earning three times their money. Then they approached me and said 'you're making the money let us close the show."

"One of our first big tours was second on the bill to Roy Orbison. It was pretty hard to keep up with that man," recalled Lennon who added, "He really put on a show ... Orbison had that fantastic voice" while Starr explained, "It was terrible following Roy. He'd slay them and they'd scream for more. As it got near to our turn we would hide behind the curtain whispering to each other 'Guess who's next folks, it's your favourite rave'."

By the time the tour entered its second week in Sheffield, the official billing had been changed and the Beatles were officially placed above Orbison on the cover of a new set of souvenir programmes although after the May 29 show in York, local reporter Stacey Brewer wrote that "Roy Orbison got the biggest 'hand' I've ever heard at the Rialto."

Now the Beatles had become both the first UK act to the bill over an American star and established themselves on a par with one of their all-time heroes who was, in turn, equally impressed by their talent. "Until now we'd never topped the bill", commented Lennon. "You can't measure success but if you could then the minute I knew we'd been successful was when Roy Orbison asked us if he could record two of our songs."

(Right) The poster from their three-week UK tour in 1963, when the Beatles topped the bill for the first time.

Ringo's jacket

Made to measure

After Manchester-born tailor Dougie A. Millings had become established as outfitter to the Beatles as a result of the revolutionary round-neck collarless suits he designed, he continued to supply them with outfits for the four of them to wear both on-stage and in 'civvy' street.

As a result of his involvement with the Beatles, the man who had dressed early British rock stars such as Cliff Richard, Tommy Steele, Billy Fury and Adam Faith became involved in designing outfits for the Kinks, the Rolling Stones and the Who – it was reported that drummer Keith Moon was wearing a Millings suit when he died in 1978.

All this resulted in Dougie Mullings and his son Gordon moving their tailoring business to new premises across Soho at 41 Great Pulteney Street and it there that they designed the outfits the Beatles took on their first tour of America in August 1964.

Mullings & Son were also responsible for numerous outfits the Beatles wore between 1960 and 1963, including Ringo's six-button double-breasted jacket. Photographs from the time show that the Beatles drummer had a penchant for natty jackets including Edwardian style frock coats and some fascinating six- and eight-buttoned designs.

Millings, who was known to the Beatles as 'Dad', due to his closeness to them all, died in 2001 but he was rewarded for his sartorial efforts on behalf of the group with a role in the group's first film *A Hard Day's Night*, in which he played a frustrated tailor.

(Above) Labels for Millings the tailors, which were individually identified and stitched into the Beatles' jackets.

(Right) Ringo Starr's double-breasted and double-buttoned jacket, made-to-measure by the Beatles' tailor.

(Right) Dougie Millings' shop front in Great Pulteney Street, with a unique Beatles-inspired window display featuring cut-outs, guitars and some alternative Beatles' song titles.

Introducing ... the Beatles **album**

An LP for the US

As a result of Capitol's reluctance to release the Beatles in America, manager Brian Epstein was free to sign over the rights to the group's first album to the US independent label Vee Jay Records and as a result an American version of 'Please Please Me' first saw the light of day in the summer of 1963.

Vee Jay Records was launched in 1953 as an off-shoot of the Chicago record shop with local acts Jimmy Reed, John Lee Hooker and the Staples Singers eventually being joined by stars such as Gene Chandler and the Four Seasons

Scheduled for release in July 1963, the album was changed dramatically for the US where albums traditionally consisted of just 12 songs. The UK title track plus 'Ask Me Why' were dropped from the album which was then re-titled *Introducing ... The Beatles* with a cover shot taken by Angus McBean which had been used on the group's 1963 British EP *The Beatles' Hits*.

Due to either a lack of success or the company's chairman using company funds to cover his gambling debts, Vee Jay was quickly forced to withdraw the album – along with titles by Frank Ifield and Alma Cogan – under pressure from EMI which in turn led to Vee Jay's deal with the British major coming to a premature end in August 1963.

However, when the Beatles began to make headlines in America, Vee Jay chose to re-issue the album on January 16, 1964 but they were then informed that the tracks 'Love Me Do' and 'P.S. I Love You' had to be removed as they were Lennon/McCartney songs which had not yet been officially released in the US and the publisher's refused to licence them to Vee Jay.

The release was subsequently delayed until February by which time, despite the official album listing not always confirming it, the tracks 'Please Please Me' and 'Ask Me Why' were seemingly re-instated on the second version of the album. The delay in releasing *Introducing ... to* American Beatles fans meant it actually became the second album by the fab four to make it into the US chart – three weeks after another re-titled and much altered collection. Eventually *Introducing ... the Beatles* rose to number two in the charts, a position it held for nine weeks during which time Vee Jay and Capitol fought out various legal battles over the US rights to Beatles' recordings.

Finally, the album which sold over 1.3 million copies in the US, reverted to Capitol in October 1964 and two years later Vee Jay, which eventually issued 'Love Me Do' in America on its subsidiary Tollie label, was finally declared bankrupt.

(Right) Released in 1963, the Beatles' first American album. This was withdrawn and then re-issued in 1964, when it finally went on to reach number two in the US charts.

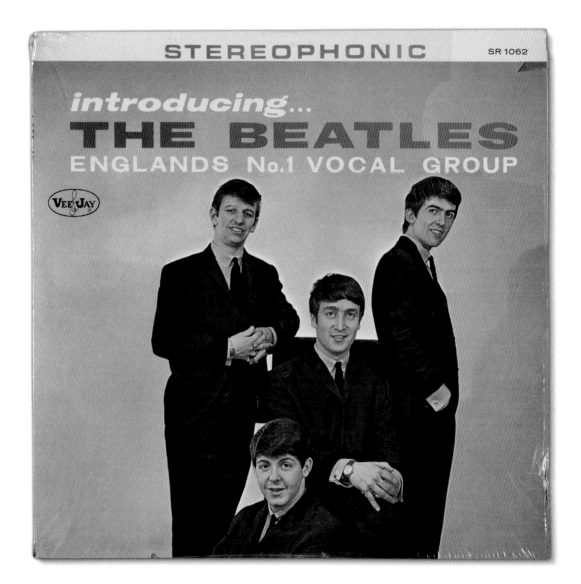

'She Loves You' promo single

This side up

When the managing director of EMI Records was presented with a manufacturing order for the Beatles' fourth single 'She Loves You' in July 1963, he was astonished at the number of records the company's marketing manager wanted to press in advance of its release.

L G Wood, the man who formally signed the group discovered by George Martin to EMI's Parlophone label, was concerned with a big order being placed in advance of EMI's annual two-week shut down in August. "He set the advance order at 350,000 which was an extraordinarily high number in those days," he remarked. "I told him I thought it was way too high but he stood his ground and eventually I agreed to 250,000 being pressed."

And, as a Wood happily recalls, "Within weeks 'She Loves You' had sold over a million." In fact the single – issued on August 23 – was the Beatles' first ever million-selling record and for over 14 years the Lennon and McCartney composition was honoured as Britain's best-selling single with total sales of over 1.6 million. It was ultimately out sold by McCartney's group Wings and their rendition of 'Mull of Kintyre' in 1977.

When 'She Loves You' was released, the copies sent to newspapers and radio and TV stations had a large red 'A' printed on the A-side to ensure that reviewers, presenters and producers focused on the right side of the single and not the B-side 'I'll Get You'.

'She Loves You' had been written by Lennon and McCartney in Newcastle-upon-Tyne on June 26, 1963 – two months before its release – in a room at the Turks Hotel where the group were staying ahead of their concert at the Majestic Ballroom. Recalling the song, McCartney said, "We must have had a few hours before the show so we said 'Oh great! Let's have a ciggy and write a song!" The band's bass player also recalls that it was "a she, you, me, I, personal preposition song" and adds, "I suppose the most interesting thing about it was that it was a message

song, it was someone bringing a message. It wasn't us anymore ... there's a little distance we managed to put in it which was quite interesting."

The song also contained a remarkable chorus of 'yeah, yeah, yeah' which quickly became a catchphrase associated with both the band and their home city of Liverpool. However, things might have been different if McCartney's father had got his way as he was all in favour of changing the chorus to 'yes, yes, yes' because he thought it was grammatically correct and sounded better.

While Lennon remembers 'She Loves You' as "Paul's idea", the two writers got together on June 27 – a day off from touring – to finish the song in McCartney's house in Forthlin Road, Liverpool. Then, four days after writing 'She Loves You', the Beatles went into Abbey Road Studios on July 1 and, during two sessions between 2.30pm and 10pm, Lennon, McCartney, Harrison and Starr recorded the song and its B-side.

Looking at the lyrics on a music stand in the studio, producer George Martin recalls being taken aback by what he saw. "I thought oh my God, what a lyric. This is going to be one that I do not like. But when they started singing it – bang, wow, terrific."

'She Loves You' was the Beatles' second successive number one in the UK and bizarrely it holds the same record in America where it followed 'I Want To Hold Your Hand' to the top spot on March 21, 1964.

While 'She Loves You' held the US top spot for just two weeks, it was number one in the UK for four weeks before slipping into the top three for seven more weeks and then re-emerging at number one for a further two weeks. It passed the one million sales milestone on November 27, 1963, during its second spell at the top of the charts.

(Right) A 1963 promotional copy of 'She Loves You', featuring a prominent red letter 'A'. This was intended to indicate which side of the record should be played and reviewed first.

PARLOPHONE

PARLOPHONE 45 R.P.M.

NORTHERN
SONGS LTD.
7XCE 17395

RECORDING FIRST
PUBLISHED 1963

R 5055

A

SHE LOVES YOU
(Lennon—McCartney)
THE BEATLES
MADE IN Gt. BRITAIN

The Parlophone Co. Ltd. All rights of the Manufacturer and of the Owner of the recorded work reserved - Unauthorised public performance, broadcasting and copying of this record prohibited

POINTS TO REMEMBER

Give E.M.I. Record Tokens (6/- to 50/-) exchangeable for all
leading makes of records ■ For latest information on the
'POPS' read the Record Mail ■ To take good care of this
record—check your stylus regularly and use 'Emitex' cleaning
material.

■ THIS RECORD MUST BE PLAYED AT 45 R.P.M. ■

E.M.I. RECORDS LTD • HAYES • MIDDLESEX • ENGLAND

Made and Printed in Great Britain

Ready, Steady, Go! invite

The weekend starts here

Britain's hippest, swinging sixties, rock and pop TV series was launched by Rediffusion Television on August 9, 1963 and was broadcast on a Friday evening throughou t the UK under the title *Ready, Steady, Go!* and with the catchphrase "the weekend starts here".

The first show, with Billy Fury as top of the bill, was hosted by TV presenter Keith Fordyce and fashion model Cathy McGowan and within two months the Beatles made their debut, miming to 'Twist And Shout', 'I'll Get You' and 'She Loves You'. In addition to the group being interviewed by singer Dusty Springfield, McCartney also judged a contest between four teenage girls who mimed to Brenda Lee's 'Let's Jump The Broomstick'.

The winner, who received her prize from the Beatles' bass player, was London girl Melanie Coe who appeared in a newspaper report in February 1967 after she ran away from home and, in a bizarre coincidence, her story seemingly inspired McCartney to compose the song 'She's Leaving Home'.

The Beatles had been in Abbey Road studios finishing off tracks for their *With the Beatles* album on the night before the October 4 TV show and immediately after their live appearance they headed off to Scotland for a three night mini tour. The 'Fab Four' were then back in the Kingsway, London studios of *Ready, Steady, Go!* on March 20, 1964 for an appearance which broke all audience viewing figures for the show which was broadcast between 6.15pm and 7pm. They performed 'It Won't Be Long', 'You Can't Do That' and 'Can't Buy Me Love' – which was released on the same day with advance orders in excess of one million – and during the show the group were presented with an award from the US music magazine Billboard in recognition of the Beatles holding the top three places on the US singles chart.

In November 1964 the Beatles appeared on the show for the third and last time when they recorded 'I Feel Fine' and 'She's A Woman', although Lennon and Harrison were later interviewed on a special *Ready, Steady, Goes Live!* edition from the programme's Wembley studios in April 1965.

After three and a half year, *Ready, Steady, Go!* aired for the last time on December 23, 1966 when the Who topped the bill but the Beatles still held the record for the largest *RSGo* audience.

(Right) Tickets for the Beatles' first (bottom) appearance on *Ready, Steady, Go!* in 1963 and their third outing in 1964, when their pre-recorded performance from November 23 was aired four days later.

(Overleaf) The Beatles rehearsing for *Ready, Steady, Go!* at the Associated-Rediffusion television studios in Kingsway, London, in March 1964.

READY, STEADY, GO!

THE BEATLES

Rediffusion London invites you to come and see at the Wembley Television Studios, Wembley Park Drive from 4.00 - 4.30 p.m. on Monday, 23rd November.

Doors open at 3.00 and close at 3.15 p.m.   No admittance under 13 years of age.

(for conditions see back)

READY, STEADY, GO!

CALLING ALL TEENAGERS ! Associated-Rediffusion invites you to come along to your show in Studio 9, Television House, Kingsway, London, W.C.2.   Friday, 4th October, 1963 6.15—7.00 p.m. Doors will be open at 5.30 p.m. No admittance under 13 years of age.

for conditions see back   THE BEATLES

Sunday Night at the London Palladium invitation

Beatlemania begins

When asked about appearing on the prestigious TV show *Sunday Night at the London Palladium* it was John Lennon who warned "There have been offers of a spot on the Palladium show but we don't feel we are ready. We have seen others go and be torn to pieces."

He added that the group "had enough cockiness" and "enough success" to justify their top billing on the show that was launched in 1955 and broadcast nationwide by ATV. On one occasion a show with Frank Ifield and Cliff Richard was watched in nearly 10 million homes around the country.

Two nights before they appeared with compere Bruce Forsyth, comedian and singer Des O'Connor and US star Brook Benton, the Beatles had performed at the Trentham Gardens Ballroom in Staffordshire. The audience for their TV appearance was estimated to be in the region of fifteen million people, who watched them perform live versions of 'I Want To Hold Your Hand', 'This Boy', 'All My Loving', 'Money' and 'Twist And Shout'.

The Beatles' appearance on October 13, 1963 at the theatre in Argyll Street in London's West End brought out such huge numbers of fans that the theatre's back-stage entrance in Great Marlborough Street was blocked and a newspaper writer used the phrase "Beatlemania" to describe the scenes. The Beatles appearance at the London Palladium prompted Starr to reflect that "there was nothing bigger in the world than making it to the Palladium" and after the group had joined in the traditional finale with all the acts waving from a revolving stage, he added, "We played *Sunday Night at the London Palladium* and we were on the roundabout and it was dynamite."

The Beatles returned to the Palladium on January 12, 1964 when they joined singer Alma Cogan and Irish comedian Dave Allen on the show and they made their third and final appearance at the theatre on July 23, 1964 as part of a special *Night Of A Thousand Stars* charity show which was held at midnight and hosted by the actor Sir Laurence Olivier. They performed a ballet sketch to the track 'I'm Flying' and were joined on the bill by stars such as Zsa Zsa Gabor, Harry Secombe, Frankie Howerd, Judy Garland and Shirley Bassey. Coincidentally, four months earlier Brian Epstein had moved his NEMS organization to offices opposite the London Palladium.

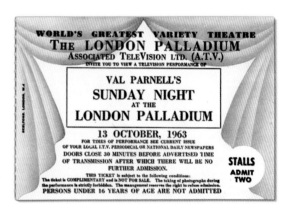

(Above) A ticket to admit two people to see The Beatles' first appearance on *Sunday Night at the London Palladium* in 1963.

(Right) Topping the bill at the London Palladium, the Beatles performed five songs and were watched by over 15 million.

Royal Variety Show programme
"Rattle your jewellery"

Just two weeks after 'She Loves You' ended its second two week spell as the UK's number one single – after its initial run of eight weeks in the top spot – the Beatles found themselves performing in front of royalty.

The *Royal Command Performance* (or *Royal Variety Show*) began way back in 1912 in front of King George V and in 1963 the show was held at the Prince of Wales Theatre in London's Coventry Street on November 4 with the Queen Mother, Princess Margaret and Lord Snowdon in attendance. The Beatles, who joined 19 other acts on the bill, took a day off between dates at the Odeon Cinema in Leeds and the Adelphi Cinema in Slough to appear in the show that was broadcast on ITV.

Impresario Bernard Delfont put the show together and, inspired by his teenager daughter's enthusiasm for the Beatles, he included them on the show alongside, among others, Marlene Dietrich, May Bygraves, Charlie Drake and Buddy Greco. They performed four songs 'She Loves You', 'Till There Was You', 'From Me To You' and 'Twist And Shout', and it was just before the last song that Lennon came out with a line that he had first suggested to manager Epstein in the dressing room.

Determined not to offend the Royal Family he had persuaded Lennon to drop the word 'fucking' from his quip and as agreed Lennon simply told the audience, "On this next number I want you all to join us. Would those in the cheap seats clap their hands. The rest can rattle your jewellery" – and even without the swear word before jewellery, the remark made the newspaper headlines. "John did his little line about 'rattle your jewellery' because the audience were all supposedly rich," said Harrison. "I think he'd spent a bit of time thinking what he could say. John also overdid the bowing as a joke because we never used to like the idea of bowing, such a showbiz thing."

After the show The Queen Mother was reported as saying "They [the Beatles] are so fresh and vital. I simply adore them" while McCartney recalled, "We met the Queen Mother and she was clapping." During the traditional after-show meet and greet, the Queen Mother apparently asked the group where they were performing next. When they told her they were due in Slough the next night, she commented, "Oh that's just near us" – a reference to the royal residence at Windsor Castle in Berkshire.

Although the Beatles made only the one appearance on the *Royal Variety Show*, they were apparently regularly invited to return but, as Lennon explained, they always turned it down. "We managed to refuse all sorts of things that people don't know about. We did the *Royal Variety Show* and we were asked discreetly to do it every year after that but we always said 'stuff it'. So every year there was a story in the newspaper 'Why No Beatles For The Queen?' which was pretty funny because they didn't know we'd refused. That show's a bad gig anyway."

(Right) The programme from the Beatles' one and only appearance on *The Royal Variety* show in 1963, when they appeared on the bill with Max Bygraves and Charlie Drake.

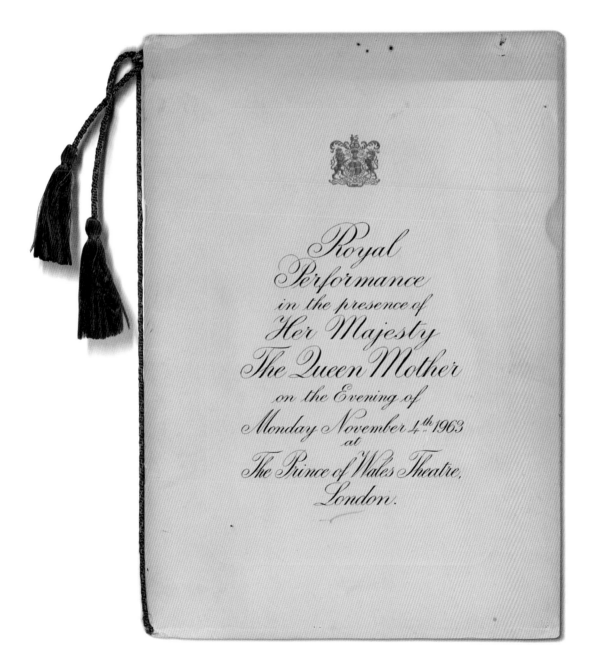

Royal
Performance
in the presence of
Her Majesty
The Queen Mother
on the Evening of
Monday November 4th 1963
at
The Prince of Wales Theatre,
London.

With the Beatles gold disc
Presented by EMI to the Fab Four and Epstein

After the success of the Beatles' debut album *Please Please Me* – and its 30-week run at number one in the British album chart – the group came up with their follow up effort *With The Beatles* and in November 1963 the new album replaced the first offering at the top of the chart and stayed there for a total of 21 weeks – which left the Beatles just one week shy of topping the UK charts for a whole year.

The Beatles returned to Abbey Road studios on July 18, 1963 – just four months after the release of their debut album – to start work on their second collection of songs. The schedule was all part of the plan hatched by manager Brian Epstein and producer George Martin to release four singles and two albums each year. By October the new album, in addition to time spent taping messages for Australian radio and making a first ever Christmas record for the Beatles fan club, was finished and it was released on November 22 with advance orders of over 300,000 and, astonishingly, the album also made a seven-week showing in the British singles chart, peaking at number 11.

With The Beatles once again came with 14 tracks but unlike its predecessor – which featured eight original songs by Lennon and McCartney and six cover versions – the new collection featured seven Lennon/McCartney songs and one track by George Harrison to go with the six covers. Despite this running order, Harrison commented that "the second album was slightly better than the first, inasmuch as we spent more time on it and there were more original songs".

For John Lennon the new album represented the group's discovery of new recording techniques. "The first set of tricks on the records was double tracking on the second album. We discovered that, or it was told to us ... and that really set the ball rolling. We double tracked ourselves off the album." The songs on *With The Beatles* once again illustrated the Beatles' love of all things American with at least three tracks coming from acts signed to the emerging Motown label – 'Please Please Mr Postman', 'You Really Got A Hold On Me' and 'Money'. "The cover songs recorded for *With The Beatles* were chosen by whoever liked them," explained Ringo Starr.

After photographer Angus McBean's effort on the first album, the Beatles turned to Robert Freeman, who had begun working with them on tour in early 1963, to come up with the idea of shooting the second album cover in black and white with the group in half shadow against a black background and wearing black sweaters. After his criticism of the cover of *Please Please Me*, Harrison was more enthusiastic about the follow-up effort. Describing it as "the first one where we thought 'hey let's get artistic'". He added, "The album cover for *With The Beatles* became one of the most copied designs of the decade.

If the album artwork was an eye-opener – and it's rumoured that EMI were reluctant to contemplate a mono cover – then the music made an even bigger impression. Alan Smith reviewed the new album for NME and suggested "If there are any Beatles-haters left in Britain, I doubt they'll remain unmoved after hearing *With The Beatles*. It's a knock-out", and he chose 'All My Loving' as "the album's highlight".

Capitol Records in America offered up *Meet The Beatles* as their equivalent of *With The Beatles*, although they dropped five of the cover versions and added 'I Want To Hold Your Hand' and 'I Saw Her Standing There'. Despite the changes the first ever album by the Beatles to be issued on EMI's US label topped the US charts in February 1964 and stayed there for 11 weeks.

(Right) One of the five special gold discs made by EMI to celebrate *With The Beatles* becoming the first album to sell one million copies in the UK.

Fan Club exclusive floppy disc

Beatles Christmas gifts

When the Beatles fan club was taken over by the group's manager Epstein – in return for him funding the operation – paid-up members then received an assortment of special offers including unique records made by the group exclusively for their fans.

It was the group's press officer Tony Barrow who came up with the idea of 'the Beatles' Fan Club Christmas Record' in an effort to satisfy the group's fans who were beginning to complain about unanswered letters and subscription payments. "No other pop or rock stars had given away a gift like this so we could bank on favourable publicity all round," was Barrow's thinking and at the same time he decided that fans of the Beatles should be referred to as 'Beatle People'.

Despite Epstein's reluctance to the idea of the special disc – "his inevitable reaction was to reject it out of hand at once on grounds of cost" says Barrow – the group were all in favour and agreed that producer George Martin could make the recording during a session in Abbey Road.

With Barrow writing a script, the Beatles recorded their first Christmas record on October 17, 1963 – after they had completed 'I Want To Hold Your Hand' – and the five minutes long flexi-disc contained 'Good King Wenceslas, John Talking, Paul Talking', 'Good King Wenceslas Ringo, George Talking', 'Good King Wenceslas George and Rudolph the Red Nosed Ringo'.

With only 25,000 copies produced – and mailed out with a newsletter which said "This record is exclusive to our Club and will not be made available elsewhere" – the first Beatles' Christmas record was, because of budget restrictions, packaged in a yellow wallet made from an inexpensive mixture of paper and board which was then stapled together. "This was the one part of the product of which I felt ashamed," said Barrow who added, "Otherwise the record did the damage limitation job ... and much more."

With the Beatles firmly on side in wanting to do more of what they called "Crimble records", the group set aside time each year to record their unique collection of carols and jokes. On October 26 1964 they spent part of the evening session in Abbey Road producing the four-minute-long *Another Beatles Christmas Record* with their own versions of 'Jingle Bells', 'Happy Christmas' and 'Can You Wash Your Father's Shirts?'

The third festive offering was recorded on November 8, 1965 – during the sessions for the *Rubber Soul* album – and was entitled *The Beatles' Third Christmas Record* and was memorable for an out-of-tune version of 'Yesterday' alongside 'Auld Lang Syne' and 'Same Old Song'. It also featured a cover photograph taken by Robert Whitaker during filing at Granada's studios for a TV special called *The Music Of Lennon and McCartney*.

A double-sided record – with the sub-title *Pantomime: Everywhere It's Christmas* – appeared in 1966 after a recording session on November 25 in the Oxford Street, London studios of music publisher Dick James. The six-minute disc included tracks called 'A Rare Cheese', 'The Feast', 'A Loyal Toast' and 'Podgy the Bear & Jasper'. *The Beatles Fifth Christmas Record* in 1967 marked the last time producer Martin would be involved – the sessions were done in Abbey Road on November 28 – as disc jockey Kenny Everett took over the task of editing the material.

It contained a front cover designed by Lennon and Starr and a painting by Julian Lennon on the back cover with guest appearances by Martin (on organ) and actor Victor Spinetti plus a specially composed song entitled 'Christmas Time (Is Here Again)' which was credited to all four members of the group.

(Right) The Beatles' first Christmas record, made especially for members of their fan club and released in 1963.

Ticket to the Beatles' Christmas show

Melodrama and music

In the run up top Christmas 1963, the Beatles found themselves booked into London's Astoria Theatre for a show that was heralded as Brian Epstein's *Fabulous Christmas Show*.

Opening on December 24, the show ran through until January 11, 1964 although the cast were given December 25 and 29 plus January 5 off and the regular two shows a night programme was changed to just one show on Christmas Eve and New Year's Eve. The 100,000 seats for the 30 shows were put up for sale on October 21 and sold out in less than a month.

The bill for the shows included Rolf Harris, who sang 'Tie Me Kangaroo Down', The Barron Knights plus four Merseyside acts which were all managed by Epstein – Cilla Black, The Fourmost, Billy J. Kramer and the Dakotas and Tommy Quickly. Midway through the show the Beatles appeared in a mock Victorian melodrama entitled *What A Night* with Lennon as Sir John Jasper, complete with false moustache, McCartney as the signalman, Harrison as Ermyntrude – in drag with a headscarf and shawl – and Starr as a snowman.

"I think we were to be congratulated for mounting a theatrical Christmas production that tried very hard to be something more than a pop concert," said the group's press officer Tony Barrow, who still had to admit that it was the songs that were really what the fans came to hear. "All that mattered in the end was the musical bit of the show, a 25 minute set at the end of the second half."

With their pantomime effort over, the Beatles in fact closed each show with a nine song set including 'Roll Over Beethoven', 'All My Loving', 'She Loves You', 'I Want To Hold Your Hand' and 'Twist And Shout'. A year later, despite being among the biggest selling act in the world, the Beatles returned to London in December 1964 for what was called *Another Beatles Christmas Show*, but this time they staged it at the Odeon Cinema in Hammersmith between December 24 and January 16, with four days off during the 20-night run.

Once again mixing music and pantomime with the constant barrage of screaming from the fans, the show featured the Yardbirds, Elkie Brooks and Freddie and the Dreamers. The takings from the show on December 29 were donated to the Brady Clubs and Settlement Charity in the East End of London.

(Right) Tickets for the Beatles' Christmas shows, which took place at the Astoria in Finsbury Park in 1963 and moved to the Hammersmith Odeon in 1964.

ASTORIA
FINSBURY PARK
BRIAN EPSTEIN presents
THE BEATLES
CHRISTMAS SHOW
1st Performance 6-40
FRIDAY
DECEMBER 27
STALLS
N17 10/-
No Tickets exchanged nor
money refunded
TO BE GIVEN UP

ASTORIA
FINSBURY PARK
BRIAN EPSTEIN presents
THE BEATLES
CHRISTMAS SHOW
1st Performance 6-40
THURSDAY
DECEMBER 26
CIRCLE
J65 10/-
No Tickets exchanged nor
money refunded
TO BE RETAINED

ODEON HAMMERSMITH
BRIAN EPSTEIN presents
ANOTHER BEATLES
CHRISTMAS SHOW
1st Performance at 6-15 p.m.
SATURDAY, DEC. 26th, 1964
STALLS 15/-
Block   Seat
21   M   12
No ticket exchanged nor money refunded
THIS PORTION TO BE RETAINED

ASTORIA
FINSBURY PARK
BRIAN EPSTEIN presents
THE BEATLES
CHRISTMAS SHOW
1st Performance 6-40
SATURDAY
DECEMBER 28
STALLS
C 5 10/-
No Tickets exchanged nor
money refunded
TO BE RETAINED

ASTORIA
FINSBURY PARK
BRIAN EPSTEIN presents
THE BEATLES
CHRISTMAS SHOW
2nd Performance 9-0
FRIDAY
DECEMBER 27
STALLS
H22 10/-
No Tickets exchanged nor
money refunded
TO BE GIVEN UP

ODEON HAMMERSMITH
BRIAN EPSTEIN presents
ANOTHER BEATLES
CHRISTMAS SHOW
2nd Performance at 8-45 p.m.
SATURDAY, DEC. 26th, 1964
STALLS £1/-/-
Block   Seat
23   D   21
No ticket exchanged nor money refunded
THIS PORTION TO BE RETAINED

ODEON HAMMERSMITH
BRIAN EPSTEIN presents
ANOTHER BEATLES
CHRISTMAS SHOW
2nd Performance at 8-45 p.m.
MONDAY, DEC. 28th, 1964
STALLS 10/-
Block   Seat
16   Z   11
No ticket exchanged nor money refunded
THIS PORTION TO BE RETAINED

ASTORIA
FINSBURY PARK
BRIAN EPSTEIN presents
THE BEATLES
CHRISTMAS SHOW
EVENING 7-0
TUESDAY
DECEMBER 31
STALLS
B16 10/-
No Tickets exchanged nor
money refunded
TO BE RETAINED

ASTORIA
FINSBURY PARK
BRIAN EPSTEIN presents
THE BEATLES
CHRISTMAS SHOW
1st Performance 6-40
MONDAY
DECEMBER 30
STALLS
E19 10/-
No Tickets exchanged nor
money refunded
TO BE GIVEN UP

ODEON HAMMERSMITH
BRIAN EPSTEIN presents
ANOTHER BEATLES
CHRISTMAS SHOW
2nd Performance at 8-45 p.m.
WED., DEC. 30th, 1964
CIRCLE 7/6
Block   Seat
3   Y   51
No ticket exchanged nor money refunded
THIS PORTION TO BE RETAINED

'I Want To Hold Your Hand', US single

Number one in America

By the time the Beatles hit number one in America, they had notched up two UK number one singles and albums. Their first major US success came with the release of what was their fifth single in their homeland and their fourth in the States.

'I Want To Hold Your Hand' was recorded in Abbey Road during two sessions during the afternoon and evening of October 17, 1963 when they also made their first Christmas record for the fan club, 'You Really Got A Hold On Me' and the single's B-side 'This Boy'. The single was completed in seven takes on a day when the studio introduced four-track recording for the first time.

Released in the UK in November, with advance orders in excess of nearly one million, it knocked the group's 'She Loves You' off the top spot and went on to sell over 1.5 million copies in Britain. Its scheduled release by EMI's American company Capitol Records – who had passed on the group's four previous singles – was set for January 13, 1964, but Washington DC-based disc jockey Carroll Baker got a copy of the record from a British airline stewardess and began playing it on air. As interest spread across America, Capitol were forced to bring forward the release to December 27, 1963 and increase the pressing order to one million.

After the group's earlier singles had been released in the US by small labels such as Vee Jay and Swan, Capitol's decision to pick up the Beatles was, according to Harrison, a career-changing moment for the group. "We knew we had a better chance of having a hit because we were finally with Capitol Records and they had to promote it. The smaller labels that had put out our earlier records didn't really promote them very much."

When 'I Want To Hold Your Hand' eventually reached number one in February 1964 – replacing Bobby Vinton's 'There! I've Said It Again' – it became the first record by a UK group to top the US chart since the Tornados' 'Telstar' almost 14 months earlier, and its seven weeks on top of the chart would be the Beatles' longest stay at the head of the US charts for over four years until 'Hey Jude' racked up nine weeks in September 1968.

On May 3, 1964 the Beatles were awarded their first American gold disc by the Recording Industry of America (RIAA) for sales of over one million copies of 'I Want To Hold Your Hand' – a song described by *Billboard* magazine as "a driving rocker with surf on the Thames sound." Assessing the importance of hitting the big time in America, Lennon said, "It just seemed ridiculous – I mean the idea of having a hit record over there. It was something you could never do."

(Above) 'I Want To Hold Your Hand', on Capitol Records, became the group's first US number one in February 1964.

(Right) The Beatles performing their million-selling UK hit single 'I Want To Hold Your Hand', ahead of its release in the US.

Pan Am signed postcard
Arriving in the Big Apple

A t 1.20pm on Friday February 7, 1964, the Beatles landed at New York's JFK airport to be greeted by an estimated 10,000 American fans who waved banners and placards welcoming the group to the US – "Welcome to Beatlesville USA" was one message.

The group had left from London's Heathrow airport on Pan Am flight 101 with manager Epstein, Cynthia Lennon and producer Phil Spector in the first class cabin plus an assortment of journalists and photographers who were also on board. Throughout the flight New York radio station WMCA broadcast up-dates on their journey across the Atlantic including announcements that it was "6.30am Beatles time" and "the temperature is 32 Beatles degrees."

The Beatles' trip to America – which came just 11 weeks after the assassination of US President John F Kennedy – prompted McCartney to wonder, "They've got their own groups. What are we going to give them that they don't already have?" while Lennon mused, "We didn't think we stood a chance."

As the passengers left the plane they were each given a Beatle kit provided by Capitol Records which consisted of a signed photo, a Beatle wig and an "I like the Beatles" badge, while 100 police officers held back the crowds as the group made their way through customs and up to the first floor of the main terminal building. There the group held a press conference for over 200 reporters and a battery of cameramen before being whisked off – in a limousine for each of them, no less – to the prestigious Plaza Hotel, overlooking Central Park in Manhattan.

According to McCartney the scenes at the airport had come as a complete surprise. "There were millions of kids at the airport which nobody had expected. We heard about it in mid-air. We thought, 'Wow! God, we have really made it'." The only one of the Beatles not to be overly excited about the reception they received at the airport was Harrison who, in addition to being the only one of the group to have visited America – "I went to New York and St Louis in 1963 to look around. I went to record stores" – was suffering with a temperature and the first symptoms of tonsillitis.

The Beatles were ensconced on the twelfth floor of the Plaza Hotel occupying the ten room Presidential Suites complex with guards on duty around the clock. There they signed fan mail, met the local media and even did a telephone interview with Brian Matthews in the UK for his Saturday Club radio show. And while TV evangelist Billy Graham told his followers that the Beatles were a "passing phase", the New York *Herald Tribune* reported that the Beatles were "all short, slight kids from Liverpool who wear four-button coats, stovepipe pants, ankle high boots with cuban heels and droll looks on their faces".

And according to Lennon, who once said about their trip to America that "we were only coming over to buy LPs", their Stateside reception came as a complete surprise. "It was just out of the dark. That's the truth, it was so out of the dark we were knocked out."

(Right) Pan American airlines flew the Beatles to America in February 1964 and the group autographed this promotional postcard during the flight.

BOEING 707 AIRLINER.

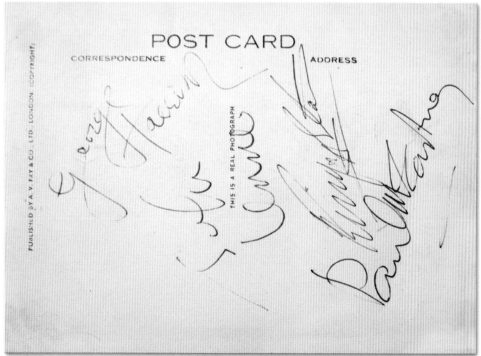

POST CARD

CORRESPONDENCE   ADDRESS

THIS IS A REAL PHOTOGRAPH

PUBLISHED BY A. V. FRY & CO. LTD. LONDON (COPYRIGHT)

(Above) When they arrived at New York's JFK airport, the Beatles were met by hordes of media and 10,000 screaming American fans.

Ticket to The Ed Sullivan Show

The biggest show on Earth

During November 1963 the Beatles' manager, Brian Epstein had been in America trying to persuade Capitol Records to issue the group's records. He was also involved in important meetings with one of the country's biggest TV stars.

Ed Sullivan was a former sports journalist and radio broadcaster before being offered his first TV show in 1948. He went on to become the host of one of America's most popular TV entertainment shows. During a trip to the UK in 1963 he and his wife experienced Beatlemania when they were at London's Heathrow airport as the Beatles returned from Sweden.

After doing his homework and finding out who the Beatles were, Sullivan met with Epstein in New York and signed the group to appear on *The Ed Sullivan Show* three times – two live and one taped performance – for a fee of $10,000 with the first appearance set for February 1964.

The Beatles had in fact been seen on US television on January 3, 1964 when NBC's Jack Paar aired a clip of the group performing 'She Loves You' taken from a BBC show called *The Mersey Sound* which had been shown in the UK in October 1963, but it was Sullivan's Sunday night prime-time show, recorded at CBS' Studio 50 in Manhattan, New York, which opened the floodgates in America.

Two days after the Beatles arrived in America for the first time, they made their much anticipated debut on US television on February 9, with Sullivan telling his audience, after he had read out a congratulatory telegram to the Beatles from Elvis Presley, "Our city, indeed our country, has never seen anything like these four young men from Liverpool. Ladies and gentlemen the Beatles!"

An estimated viewing audience of over 73 million – in addition to the 728 people seated in the TV studio (50,000 people applied for tickets to the show) – then sat and watched as the Beatles played live 'All My Loving', 'Till There Was You', 'She Loves You', 'I Saw Her Standing There' and 'I Want To Hold Your Hand', which had reached number one in America the previous week. Despite suffering from tonsillitis and flu, George Harrison made it to the studios to perform on the show and later reflected, "We were aware that Ed Sullivan was the big one because we got a telegram from Elvis and the Colonel. And I've heard that while the show was on there were no reported crimes or very few. When the Beatles were on Ed Sullivan even the criminals had a rest for ten minutes."

McCartney also understood the importance of the show to the development of the Beatles in America. "Seventy three million people were reported to have watched the first show. It was very important. We came out of nowhere with funny hair, looking like marionettes or something. That was very influential. I think that was really one of the big things that broke us."

Renowned for the record-breaking figures achieved for an appearance by Elvis Presley in 1956, Sullivan's show reached a new high with the 73 million who watched the Beatles on February 9. Many of them tuned in again a week later to watch the Beatles perform 'She Loves You', 'This Boy', 'All My Loving', 'I Saw Her Standing There', 'From Me To You' and 'I Want To Hold Your Hand' on a show broadcast from Florida. On February 23 the Beatles featured on *The Ed Sullivan Show* for the third week running when a performance of 'Twist And Shout', 'Please Please Me' and 'I Want To Hold Your Hand', taped before their debut appearance, was broadcast.

(Right) One of the 728 tickets issued for the Beatles' first appearance on *The Ed Sullivan Show* in New York.

CBS Studio 50
Presents

THE ED SULLIVAN SHOW

FEBRUARY 9, 1964

— ADMIT ONE —

(Left) Media and studio crew look on as Ed Sullivan (second left) embraces Paul McCartney and George Harrison after the Beatles' appearance on his prime time TV show.

Washington Coliseum poster
The first show in the USA

When the Beatles eventually made their live debut in America it was in the unlikely setting of an indoor sports arena normally used for basketball, boxing and ice skating. On February 11, 1964, two days after their TV debut on *The Ed Sullivan Show*, the Beatles travelled south by train from New York's Penn Street station to Washington DC after abandoning plans to fly because of a snowstorm.

The Washington Coliseum was opened in 1941 and became home to the basketball teams Washington Capitols and Washington Caps. Located close to the US capital city's Union Station, the Coliseum boasted a capacity of around 9,000 seats and was chosen to be the venue for the Beatles' February 11 show during their two city trips to the US which saw them returning to New York for shows at Carnegie Hall on February 12.

The group stepped on to the stage at The Coliseum at around 8.30pm in front of just over 8,000 people who paid between $2 and $4 for a seat to see the Beatles play in the round on a revolving stage. Following British female duo the Caravelles, American girl group the Chiffons and singer Tommy Roe, Lennon, McCartney, Harrison and Starr played 'Roll Over Beethoven', From 'Me To You', 'I Saw Her Standing There', 'This Boy', 'All My Loving', 'I Wanna be Your Man', 'Please Please Me', 'Till There Was You', 'She Loves You', 'I Want To Hold Your Hand', 'Twist And Shout' and 'Long Tall Sally' to non-stop screams while being pelted by jelly babies – much to Harrison's annoyance.

"They hurt. They don't have soft jelly babies in America but hard jelly babies like bullets."

Beatles roadie Neil Aspinall recalled that the Beatles' first show in America was far from perfect. "The Washington show was difficult because they were in a boxing ring with the audience all around and they had to play to all four sides."

Starr, who was on a round turntable in the middle of the stage which also had to turn to face all sides, had a recollection of the American experience. "What happened in the States was just like Britain only ten times bigger", said the drummer before over-estimating the size of the crowd. "The first Washington crowd was 20,000. We'd only been used to 2000 at home."

After their first ever live concert in America, the Beatles were whisked off to a party at the British Embassy in Washington DC where the group fell out with embassy staff and guests who demanded autographs and even attempted to cut their hair. "The Beatles loathed that reception", said manager Epstein, "Since then we have refused every invitation of that type."

(Right) This hand bill offered fans another chance to see the Beatles' show at Washington Coliseum in February for $2 on a twice-daily big screen broadcast in March 1964.

(Below) A $2.50 ticket to see a closed circuit broadcast of the Beatles first American concert in California – a month after it took place.

(Overleaf) The Beatles on stage in front of over 8,000 people during their debut US concert in Washington DC in February 1964.

YOU AIN'T SEEN or heard NOTHIN' YET!
IN FULL CONCERT...
A GREAT NEW SHOW!
CLOSED CIRCUIT-
BIG SCREEN!
NATIONAL GENERAL CORPORATION
PRESENTS
THE BEATLES
(CAPITOL RECORDING ARTISTS)
DIRECT FROM THEIR
FIRST AMERICAN CONCERT
IN
WASHINGTON D.C., COLISEUM!
DO NOT CONFUSE WITH HOME TV!
Produced by Concerts, Inc.
LUCKY NUMBER
Nº 4740
YOU MAY WIN A FREE ALBUM!
(BRING This AD To THEATRE)
And on the Same Show!
"THE BEACH BOYS"
AMERICA'S SURFING-SINGING SENSATIONS!
LESLEY GORE
SHE'S THE NATION'S No. 1 TEENAGE SINGING SWEETHEART!
SATURDAY
SUNDAY
March 14-15
Two Matinee Performances Each Day! In Theatres...Nationwide!
2 SHOWS DAILY . . . at 11:30 a.m. & 2:00 p.m.
ALL SEATS - - $2.00 (TAX INCLUDED)
SAN MATEO Theatre
64 E. THIRD AVE.
SAN MATEO
TICKETS NOW ON SALE!
No Reserved Seats . . . .
Only House Capacity Sold.
YOUR ADVANCE TICKET PURCHASE ASSURES YOU A SEAT!

Billboard chart, April 4, 1964

Five in the top five

When the Beatles hit the top spot in the US singles chart for the third time with 'Can't Buy Me Love' in April 1964, they became the first act to have records in the top five positions of the *Billboard* chart.

The issue of America's leading music industry magazine which carried the chart for the week ending April 4 showed 'Can't Buy Me Love' at number one, followed by 'Twist And Shout', 'She Loves You', 'I Want To Hold Your Hand' and 'Please Please Me' as the five best-selling singles in America. This was – and remains – a record for the US charts and followed the Beatles having the top four singles the previous week.

The rise of 'Can't Buy Me Love' to number one also set a record when it became the first record to jump to the spot from outside the top 20 – moving up from number 27 to number one in just two weeks. The same single also gave the Beatles the record as the first act to have three successive number one hits – beating Elvis Presley's two consecutive chart-toppers in 1956.

The international advance orders for 'Can't Buy Me Love' ran to a record-breaking 2.1 million and sales in its first week of release were well over three million with

the US accounting for 2 million, and a further 1.2 million coming from the UK where it topped the chart in the same week as America.

And it didn't end there as the following week, with 'Can't Buy Me Love' still at number one, the Beatles could claim a further 13 positions on the chart with singles at 2, 4, 7, 9, 14, 38, 48, 50, 52, 61, 74, 78 and 81. This gave them the greatest ever monopoly of the US singles chart since Presley had nine records in the chart in 1956.

A week earlier the Beatles had gone one better in Australia when 'I Saw Her Standing There', 'Love Me Do', 'Roll Over Beethoven', 'All My Loving', 'She Loves You' and 'I Want To Hold Your Hand' took the top six places in the country's singles chart.

After five weeks at number one in America, 'Can't Buy Me Love' was replaced by Louis Armstrong's 'Hello Dolly' – although they still had 'Do You Want To Know A Secret' at number two – while in the UK it was knocked off the number one spot by Peter & Gordon's version of the Lennon and McCartney song 'World Without Love', which also went to number one in America in June 1964.

(Right) Billboard's Hot 100 chart from April 4, 1964, with the Beatles setting a never-to-be-beaten record by holding the top five positions, ahead of Terry Stafford and Louis Armstrong.

George's Asahi Pentax camera
Smile for the camera

For nearly ten years John Lennon, Paul McCartney, George Harrison and Ringo Starr lived out their lives as Beatles in front of the cameras. Whether it was official photographers, a news cameraman or just the fans, the clamour for a snap of the fab four was a never ending aspect of their daily lives.

The demand for pictures of the Beatles took its toll on the group, as Starr once recounted: "You got to a club and there's some little photographer with big cameras and none of them say 'Can I take your picture?' They run up and put their flash about four inches from your eyes." However, it seems that being constantly photographed might just have stirred an interest in cameras and photography in the Beatles themselves, as McCartney captured Harrison and Starr on camera in 1963 during a holiday in Tenerife. He was there once again with his camera in 1966 when the Beatles visited both India and America.

Starr, who was famously filmed with a camera around his neck for some scenes in the movie *A Hard Day's Night*, also became a keen photographer and was captured showing his equipment to French singer Sylvie Vartan in 1964 and turning up at the hospital – camera at the ready – to get a first picture of his son Jason when he was born in August 1967.

It also seems that Harrison, famously the most camera shy of the Beatles, was also a fan of the camera and worked with Lennon on producing "a little 8mm film" when they went on holiday with their wives to Tahiti in May 1964. Together with McCartney, he also indulged in a game of photographing themselves in hotel room mirrors before being photographed by 'official' Beatles photographer Robert Whittaker experimenting with a Poloraid 100 instant camera during an unscheduled stopover in Alaska in 1966.

Harrison bought his Asahi Pentax some time in the early 1960s and was seen using it in 1964 and also pictured with it – as well as two other cameras – round his neck on what seems to be an airport runway.

The black-bodied camera, which was launched by Pentax in 1960, was given by Harrison to his father Harold, who died in 1978, and it then passed on to his eldest brother Harry, who eventually became estate manager on Harrison's Friar Park home in Berkshire, before the camera was put up for sale at an auction of many of Harrison's personal items in 2012.

(Right) Keen photographer George Harrison's favourite Pentax camera, which he passed on to his father and then later gave to his brother.

(Overleaf) While Ringo Starr catches up on some reading, George Harrison shows off his Pentax camera to a fellow passenger during one of the Beatles' many plane journeys.

US Tour itinerary
27 dates on an envelope

Six months after the Beatles made their first ever appearances in America – two Ed Sullivan TV shows coupled with concerts in Washington and New York – the group returned to the US in August 1964 for a 25-date tour of the States. Manager Brian Epstein jotted down the itinerary on an old envelope dated March 25, 1964 – the day when the Beatles appeared on BBC TV's *Top Of The Pops* for the first time performing 'Can't Buy Me Love'.

While the Beatles were working on *A Hard Day's Night* – creating the music in the studio and out on location filming the movie – Epstein was presumably planning the details of the group's month-long tour of America which opened on August 19 at the Cow Palace in San Francisco where they were supported by the Righteous Brothers, Jackie de Shannon and the Exciters and earned a £17,000 share of gate receipts that were worth over £32,000.

Exactly as Epstein noted down on the envelope he received from the *Daily Express* newspaper, the Beatles moved on to play concerts in Las Vegas – where the shows were twice stopped because fans were hurling jelly babies at the stage – and at Los Angeles's famous Hollywood Bowl. They then moved on to perform in New York, Atlantic City, Philadelphia, Chicago and in to Canada for shows in Toronto and Montreal.

Back in the States, the Beatles arrived for a show in Jacksonville, Florida which they and their manager had initially refused to play unless they were given an assurance that the audience would not be colour segregated. In the event, 9,000 of the 32,000 ticket holders couldn't get to the auditorium because of damage caused by Hurricane Dora. At the show on September 15 in Cleveland there was trouble of another sort when a bunch of fans broke through the police cordon and invaded the stage causing the show to be stopped and the Beatles to be escorted from the stage.

Two nights later the Beatles played an extra show which was not included on Epstein's original list but proved to be a good bit of business as the September 17 concert at Kansas City's Municipal Stadium earned the Beatles a world record fee of $150,000.

As planned, the tour came to an end in New York on September 20 with a charity show at the Paramount Theatre in aid of Retarded Infants Service and Cerebal Palsy of New York.

The Beatles were joined on the bill by other stars, including the Tokens, Bobby Goldsboro, the Shangri-Las, Steve Lawrence and Edie Gorme and Jackie DeShannon, while Bob Dylan visited the group backstage. The show attracted a sell-out audience of 3,682 people, paying between 5 and 100 dollars a ticket and raised over £25,000 for charity.

(Above) The Beatles on stage at San Francisco's Cow Place, during the opening show of the 1964 US tour.

(Right) Brian Epstein's original hand-written itinerary for the Beatles' tour of America and Canada

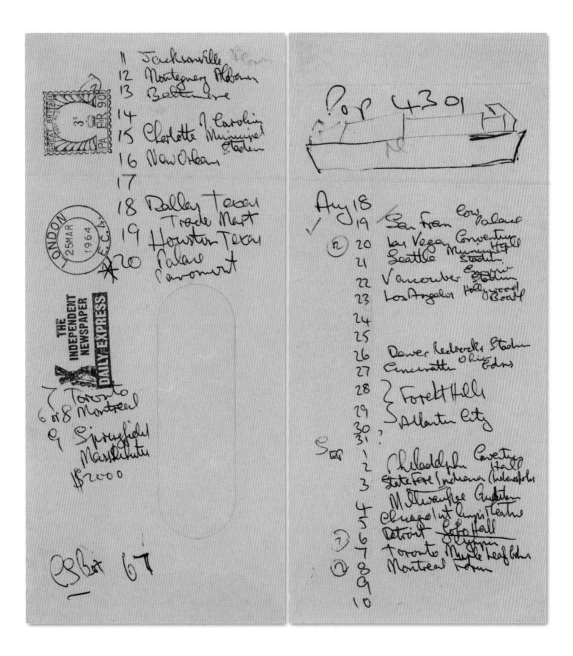

11 Jacksonville Fla
12 Montgomery Alabam
13 Baltimore
14 Charlotte N Carolina
15 Charlotte Municipal
                Stadium
16 New Orleans
17
18 Dalley Texas
        Trade Mart
19 Houston Texas
20 Palace
        Paramount

LONDON 25 MAR 1964 E.C.4.

THE INDEPENDENT NEWSPAPER
DAILY EXPRESS

6 7 Toronto
    8 Montreal
9 Springfield
    Massachusetts
$2000

CSBt 6 7
1

Pop 430

Aug 18
    19 San Fran Cow Palace
    20 Las Vegas Convention
    21 Seattle Municipal Hall
                    Stadium
    22 Vancouver Empire Stadium
    23 Los Angeles Hollywood Bowl
    24
    25
    26 Denver Redrocks Stadium
    27 Cincinatti Ohio Edns
    28 } Forest Hills
    29 } Atlantic City
    30
    31 ?
Sep
    1 Philadelphia Convention Hall
    2 State Fare Indiana Indianapolis
    3 Milwaukee Auditorium
    4 Chicago Int Amphitheatre
    5 Detroit Olympia
    6 Lofa Hall
    7 Toronto Maple Leaf Gdns
    8 Montreal Forum
    9
    10

In His Own Write

Signed by John, Paul, George and Ringo

"When the group started going on the road I used to take out my typewriter after the show and just tap away as the fancy took me," was John Lennon's explanation behind the creation of his first book.

His collection of nonsense verse and rhymes entitled *In His Own Write* was published on March 23, 1964 as a pocket sized hard book with a cover photograph of Lennon taken by the Beatles' regular photographer Robert Freeman.

Published in the UK by Jonathan Cape, the book included some of the writings and drawings Lennon had created at school and for *Mersey Beat* magazine alongside later items. "An awful lot of the material was written while were on tour, most of it when we were in Margate [the Beatles played the seaside town for a week in July 1963]," said Lennon.

Described by the writer as being "about nothing" and "just meant to be funny", the book sold over 100,000 copies and quickly topped the British best-sellers list before being published in the US on April 27, just four days after Lennon had been guest of honour at the prestigious Foyle's literary lunch organized by the London book seller on the 400th anniversary of William Shakespeare's birth.

Manager Epstein recalled that the Beatle went along to celebrate the success of his book but refused to make any sort of speech although he did grab the microphone and tell the assembled guests, "Thank you all very much, you've got a lucky face."

The prestigious American magazine *Time* suggested that Lennon was "an unlikely heir to the English tradition of literary nonsense" while his collection of works, which reflected his fascination with writers such as Lewis Carroll, Edward Lear and James Thurber, was described by the *Times Literary Review* as "Worth the attention of anyone who fears for the impoverishment of the English language."

After appearing with Pete Cook and Dudley Moore on their satirical BBC TV programme *Not Only ... But Also* in January 1965, when he read some of his poetry, Lennon published his second book on June 24, 1965. *A Spaniard In the Works* was again published by Jonathan Cape and was once again a best-selling title.

Considered less cruel and more adult, the second book was published in America in July 1965 and later the two titles were brought together by Penguin in a combined publication titled *The Penguin John Lennon*. Costing 7s.6d (37p), the paperback featured Lennon in a 'superman' pose on the cover which was created by Alan Aldridge who was a popular 'swinging sixties' graphic designer.

Lennon admitted, "There's a wonderful feeling about doing something successfully other than singing. I don't suppose the royalties will ever amount to much, but it doesn't matter. I like writing books."

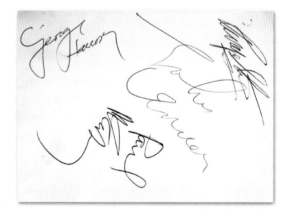

(Above) All four Beatles signed a blank page in John Lennon's first book, published in 1964.
(Right) *In His Own Write*, which was published in March and took Lennon to the top of the best-sellers list.

JOHN LENNON

IN HIS OWN WRITE

Madame Tussauds waxworks
Spot the difference!

On March 28, 1964 the Beatles became the first pop stars to be modelled in wax and put on show at the world famous Madame Tussauds exhibition in London.

They were unveiled to the public and the media at the wax museum in London's Marylebone Road wearing a set of the grey round-collar 'Beatles' suits designed and made by tailor Dougie Millings just a year earlier. On April 29 the Beatles, before they headed off to Scotland for a show in Edinburgh, paid a visit to Madame Tussauds to be photographed with their likenesses.

Wax models of the Beatles were on show at the museum for four years through to 1968. They were given five changes of outfits, including the versions wearing the suits which appeared on the front cover of their *Sgt Pepper's Lonely Hearts Club Band* album, when they stood alongside other wax images – Sonny Liston, Diana Dors, Lawrence of Arabia and George Bernard Shaw – borrowed from Tussauds. The sleeve's designer Sir Peter Blake subsequently bought the model of American boxer Liston.

Madame Anne Marie Tussaud was born in France in 1761 and modelled her first figure – French writer Voltaire – in 1771. She set up her original exhibition of wax models in London in 1802 and opened her London museum in Marylebone Road in 1844. Destroyed by fire in 1925, it re-opened in 1928 and over the years additional museums have opened in the UK, America and Japan.

(Above) A set of 'original' waxwork models of the Beatles' heads (and Ringo's hand), which went on display in 2005.

(Right) The Beatles (front) with their first waxwork models, which were unveiled at Madame Tussauds in 1964.

Japanese singles
A rush-release

A month after the Beatles' domination of the US single charts, the world's second biggest music market finally released the group's 45rpm offerings for the first time – and they did it in a bit of a rush.

On May 2, 1964 EMI's Japanese partners Toshiba issued 'I Want To Hold Your Hand' as the first single from the Beatles to be released in Japan. On the very next day they put out 'Please Please Me' and on May 4 they issued three more records – 'She Loves You', 'Can't Buy Me Love' and 'From Me To You' – and finally on May 5 they brought the total of new Beatles singles up to nine with the release of 'Twist & Shout', 'Do You Want To Know a Secret', 'All My Loving' and 'Please Mr Postman'.

All the singles were issued on the Odeon label and most appeared in picture bags which were unheard of in the UK except for EPs and the Japanese later released 'Twist & Shout' as the first Beatles EP in August 1964. Even though the group had not toured Japan in 1964, they were already popular and the mass release of the nine singles came just a month after *Meet the Beatles* was issued as the group's debut album in Japan.

While consisted of 14 tracks – just as the first two British albums and unlike the reduced American versions – the collection of songs included six from the UK's *Please Please Me* album, five from the follow-up release *With The Beatles* plus the singles 'I Want To Hold Your Hand', 'She Loves You' and 'From Me To You'.

Over the years Japan has built up a collection of Beatles releases unequalled anywhere else in the world with virtually all the UK albums and the US titles being released alongside a handful of locally created collections.

The Beatles finally visited Japan in June and July 1966 to play five concerts at the Nippon Budokan Hall in Tokyo over three nights and to a total of 50,000 fans who, according to McCartney were "very well behaved compared to what we'd seen of Western crowds" and greeted the group in their own unique way. "They sang a song that went 'Hello Beatles! Welcome Beatles!' – something pretty naff in rock 'n' roll terms but it was very nice of them to do it."

It turned out that the Japanese were fortunate to see the Beatles in the summer of 1966 as, armed with farewell gifts of Nikon cameras from the local promoter, they flew on to the Philippines and then on to America to play their last ever live concerts.

(Above) The Japanese edition of 'She Loves You'.
(Right) Two more – 'Can't Buy Me Love' and 'I Want To Hold Your Hand' – of the nine Beatles singles released in Japan in just four days in May 1964.
(Overleaf) The Beatles on stage at Tokyo's Nippon Budokan Hall.

A Hard Day's Night call sheet

A big screen debut

On March 2, 1964 the Beatles began shooting their big screen debut on a at Twickenham Studios and on location in and around London. Working with a budget of £200,000, producer Walter Shenson and director Dick Lester hired Liverpool writer Alun Owen to produce the script with photographer Robert Freeman in charge of the opening credits and George Martin as musical director.

During the two months the Beatles spent making the film, they visited a variety of locations including Marylebone Railway Station, a field near Gatwick Airport in Sussex, La Scala Theatre in London's Charlotte Street plus streets in the Notting Hill district of London. The scenes on a train were shot during a journey between London and Minehead, while Ringo Starr's solo moments were filmed in Kew, close to the Twickenham film set.

At the outset the film didn't have a firm title and while *Beatlemania, On The Move* and *Let's Go* were all considered, the final choice of *A Hard Day's Night* was down to either Starr or Lennon – depending on which story you prefer.

The group's drummer was famous for his odd quotes and quips and he is credited with saying, after a long day's work, that it had been 'a hard day's night' and this comment has been cited as the inspiration for the film's title by many including producer Shenson. However Lennon, in his book *In His Own Write*, published on March 23, 1964, wrote a line about a character who had "had a hard day's night".

Once the title had been agreed, the Beatles then had to go away and write a song to go over the opening sequence and link up with the tracks they had already composed for the film soundtrack which they began recording in early March. The non-soundtrack songs were recorded in the first week of June and on July 10 the album was released.

With a cast featuring Wilfred Brambell, Victor Spinetti, Norman Rossington and John Junkin, *A Hard Day's Night* – with Harrison's future wife Pattie Boyd cast as a schoolgirl – earned over $14 million on its initial release and foreign language versions were released in Italy, Germany, France and Holland. The critics were also favourable, one saying there had been "Nothing like it since the Goons on radio and the Marx Brothers in the thirties" and another saying it was "as funny as the Marx Brothers".

However, when the Beatles saw the film, Lennon commented, "The first time we saw it was the worst because there were producers and directors of the film all there" and then added, "By the end of the film we didn't know what had happened and we hated it."

(Right) All four Beatles signed this copy of a call sheet for scenes from the film *A Hard Day's Night*, which were shot in La Scala theatre in London in March 1964, when everybody had a call time – except for the Beatles.

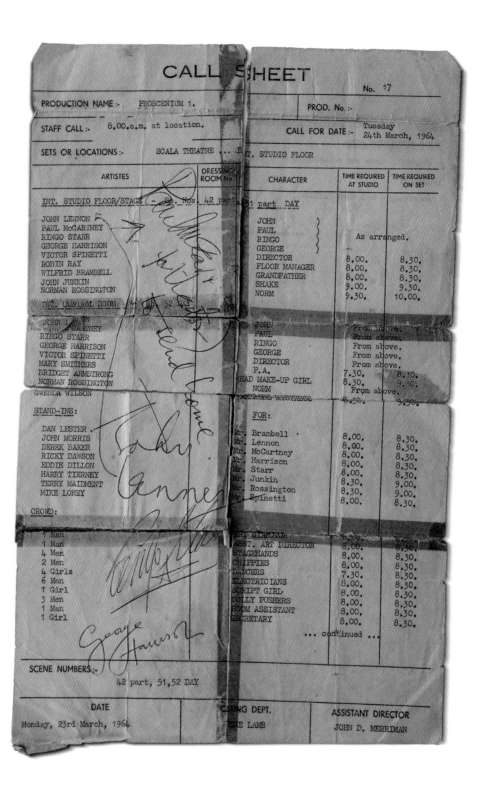

CALL SHEET

No. 17

PRODUCTION NAME :-	PROSCENIUM 1.		PROD. No. :-	

STAFF CALL :- 8.00.a.m. at location.

CALL FOR DATE :- Tuesday 24th March, 1964

SETS OR LOCATIONS :- SCALA THEATRE ... INT. STUDIO FLOOR

ARTISTES	DRESSING ROOM No	CHARACTER	TIME REQUIRED AT STUDIO	TIME REQUIRED ON SET
INT. STUDIO FLOOR/STAGE - Sc. Nos. 42 part, 51 part DAY				
JOHN LENNON		JOHN	⎫	
PAUL McCARTNEY		PAUL	⎪	
RINGO STARR		RINGO	⎬ As arranged.	
GEORGE HARRISON		GEORGE	⎭	
VICTOR SPINETTI		DIRECTOR	8.00.	8.30.
ROBIN RAY		FLOOR MANAGER	8.00.	8.30.
WILFRID BRAMBELL		GRANDFATHER	8.00.	8.30.
JOHN JUNKIN		SHAKE	9.00.	9.30.
NORMAN ROSSINGTON		NORM	9.30.	10.00.
INT. CONTROL ROOM - Sc. No. 52 DAY				
JOHN LENNON		JOHN	From above.	
PAUL McCARTNEY		PAUL	From above.	
RINGO STARR		RINGO	From above.	
GEORGE HARRISON		GEORGE	From above.	
VICTOR SPINETTI		DIRECTOR	From above.	
MARY SMITHERS		P.A.	7.30.	8.30.
BRIDGET ARMSTRONG		HEAD MAKE-UP GIRL	8.30.	9.30.
NORMAN ROSSINGTON		NORM	From above.	
GWENDA WILSON		WARDROBE MISTRESS	8.30.	9.30.
STAND-INS :		FOR :		
DAN LESTER		Mr. Brambell	8.00.	8.30.
JOHN MORRIS		Mr. Lennon	8.00.	8.30.
DEREK BAKER		Mr. McCartney	8.00.	8.30.
RICKY DAWSON		Mr. Harrison	8.00.	8.30.
EDDIE DILLON		Mr. Starr	8.00.	8.30.
HARRY TIERNEY		Mr. Junkin	8.30.	9.00.
TERRY MAIDMENT		Mr. Rossington	8.30.	9.00.
MIKE LONEY		Mr. Spinetti	8.00.	8.30.
CROWD :				
1 Man		ART DIRECTOR	8.00.	8.30.
1 Man		ASST. ART DIRECTOR	8.00.	8.30.
4 Men		STAGEHANDS	8.00.	8.30.
2 Men		CHIPPIES	8.00.	8.30.
4 Girls		DANCERS	7.30.	8.30.
6 Men		ELECTRICIANS	8.00.	8.30.
1 Girl		SCRIPT GIRL	8.00.	8.30.
3 Men		DOLLY PUSHERS	8.00.	8.30.
1 Man		ROOM ASSISTANT	8.00.	8.30.
1 Girl		SECRETARY	8.00.	8.30.
		... continued ...		

SCENE NUMBERS :-
42 part, 51,52 DAY

DATE	CASTING DEPT.	ASSISTANT DIRECTOR
Monday, 23rd March, 1964	IRENE LAMB	JOHN D. MERRIMAN

Invitation to *A Hard Day's Night* supper party

Fit for a Princess

Four days before the release of the album *A Hard Day's Night*, the Beatles' first film was given a Royal World Premiere at the London Pavilion cinema in front of Princess Margaret and the Earl of Snowdon, while the crowds forced the closure of Piccadilly Circus and the surrounding streets. A second 'premiere' took place in Liverpool at the Odeon Cinema on July 10 – almost three weeks before the film went on general release in the UK – and it was premiered at the Beacon Theatre in New York on August 12 and the opened in 500 American theatres the next day.

With half a dozen hit records to their name – and more in America – plus headline tours and major TV appearances under their belts, the Beatles and their manager Brian Epstein decided it was time to go one step further and move into the world of films. "For a while we had been thinking about making a film", said McCartney. "We had progressed to success in America. Now it was a film."

American film company United Artists decided to offer the Beatles and Epstein a three-film deal, primarily in order to get them on to the UA record label in America. They eventually hired Shenson as producer and he chose Lester to be the director. In their negotiations with Epstein, UA were prepared to offer the Beatles 25% of the net profits from the film but were taken aback by Epstein's initial demand for just 7.5%.

However, by the time the deal was signed and first announced to the public in December 1963, Epstein's legal representative had got it back to 25% although McCartney it seems was unaware of the terms. "I don't know what the exact deal was for the movie but I recall we didn't get a royalty. We were given a flat fee. Looking back it would have been better to have taken a small percentage."

And in addition to the instant success of the film, the album *A Hard Day's Night*, which was the first to consist entirely of songs written by John Lennon and Paul McCartney (although not all the tracks on the album appeared in the movie), stayed at number one in the UK for 21 weeks and spent 14 weeks at the top of the US chart. In Britain the album eventually gave up the number one spot to the follow-up Beatles album *Beatles For Sale* while the title track single also topped the charts in both the UK and US.

(Above) Tickets to the Royal World Premiere of the Beatles' film *A Hard Day's Night*.

(Right) The lavish invitation to the *A Hard Day's Night* post-premiere supper party at London's Dorchester Hotel.

Supper Party

following

Royal World Premiere

"A Hard Day's Night"

The Dorchester
Park Lane W.1

Monday, 6th July, 1964

Liverpool Airport overcrowding notice
Going back home

When the Beatles returned from their first trip to America in February 1964, over 3,000 fans assembled at London's Heathrow airport in the early hours of a Saturday morning to greet their heroes.

From the airport's Kingsford-Suite, the Beatles gave a press conference which later featured in a most unlikely television programme. BBC TV's main weekend sports magazine show was *Grandstand* and during its broadcast spot between 1pm and 5.15pm on a Saturday afternoon, footage from the conference was shown alongside an interview with the host and sports commentator David Coleman.

As a result – in between introducing horse racing, rugby league and amateur boxing and ahead of the day's football results – Coleman also conducted a 13-minute interview with the Beatles from London Airport while reporter Polly Elwes spoke to the fans who had arrived to see the group's return to the UK.

Five months later – on July 10, 1964 – the Beatles made another triumphant return when they flew from London to Liverpool Airport for a civic reception at the city's Town Hall and to attend the Northern premier of their film *A Hard Day's Night* at the Odeon cinema.

Over 200,000 loyal Beatle fans lined the route from the airport to the city centre and Paul McCartney observed, "We landed at the airport and found there were crowds everywhere" and went on to say, "It was incredible because people were lining the streets that we'd known as children, that we'd taken the bus down or walked down. And here we were now with thousands of people – for us."

The plane journey back to Liverpool had an impact on George Harrison who recalled that when they first flew in and out of their local airport, they travelled on some pretty basic planes before adding, "I think by the time we went up for the premier they'd started using the Dakota turbo-prop planes."

The arrival of the Beatles at Liverpool Airport, which had opened as Speke Airport in 1930 and was known as RAF Speke during World War II, on a Saturday afternoon in July forced the local Liverpool Corporation, who took over the running of the airport in 1961, to close their public lounge area for two hours as a safety precaution.

In 1986, ten years after the airport had been privatized, the original terminal at Liverpool Airport was replaced with a new building and in March 2002 Liverpool Airport was officially renamed John Lennon Airport. The opening ceremony – which took place 22 years after Lennon's death in New York – involved Yoko Ono and Cherie Booth, wife of British Prime Minister Tony Blair, in the unveiling of a bronze statue of Lennon. At the same time the words "Above us only sky" – from Lennon's song 'Imagine' – were put on permanent display in the roof of the main airport building.

(Right) A signed copy of Liverpool Airport's closure announcement from 1964 (top), and Yoko Ono at the opening of John Lennon Airport in Liverpool, 38 years later.

Beatles record player

From bread rolls to wallpaper

Brian Epstein was always reluctant to be seen as a manager who exploited his acts for money but as the Beatles turned into a brand that could be used to sell a range of products to their ever increasing number of fans, he was forced to enter the world of merchandising.

Following the launch of *Beatles Monthly* in July 1963 and its link with the fan club, Epstein allowed advertisements to be placed in the magazine in March 1964 offering Beatles jumpers at 35/- (£1.75) and badges for 6d (2½p), which were available by mail order from a company run by cousins. The manager was keen to retain personal 'quality control' when it came to Beatles products but as his NEMS empire grew ever bigger he found it more and more difficult to maintain his close involvement.

In an effort to continue to raise revenue which could be added to the Beatles' performance income and record royalties, Epstein eventually turned over control of the merchandising business to his lawyer David Jacobs. As the number of enquiries from companies anxious to manufacture Beatles-related products continued to grow, Jacobs concluded a number of deals in the UK that he took to Epstein and the Beatles for final approval.

They allowed Mobil Oil to sell photographs of the Beatles at their garages in Australia for a single payment of £2,000; a licence was granted to a bakery in Liverpool allowing them to make 'Ringo Rolls' for a royalty of one old penny per roll; and a London-based company made metal trays which sold for 5s 9d (28p) and earned the Beatles 2½d (1 new pence) per tray. A business in Manchester produced Beatles wallpaper costing 14s 6d (72½p) a roll while ottomans, record players, chewing gum, bedspreads and toy guitars were just some of the products made under licence.

However, when it came to America – where one company imported 10 million sticks of liquorice rock with the Beatles' name printed throughout from a company in Blackpool – Jacobs and Epstein made a monumental and costly mistake. They decided to sign away the US merchandising rights to a young man called Nicky Byrne and his partners who quickly established a company called Seltaeb (Beatles backwards), which concluded a deal in 1964 giving them 90% of the income and left NEMS and the Beatles with just 10%.

While Epstein's honesty was never in doubt, there were hints that his negotiating skills – particularly in new areas such as merchandising and film making – had let the Beatles down. Lennon once commented, "But on the business end, Brian ripped us off on the Seltaeb thing."

Pete Brown, an assistant in Epstein's NEMS store in Liverpool who went on to become a director of both NEMS and Apple, suggested that while his old boss was "one of the most honest managers in the industry", there were aspects of the business that he found hard to understand. "The idea of merchandising, music publishing and record deals – it was all new territory."

Although merchandising was in its infancy in the early 1960s, the Beatles were very much at the vanguard of a new business and sales of wigs, shirts, cookies, popsicles, purses, belts, key-rings, wallpaper, toothbrushes, dolls and towels in America ran into millions. The Wall Street Journal once estimated that the income from Beatles merchandising in 1964 would have topped $50 million.

Eventually the deal between NEMS and Seltaeb became a personal issue for Epstein, who felt he had let the Beatles down. He was drawn into a series of law suits and counter claims covering conflicts of interest, increased percentages, audits damages and even libel, which were eventually settled when NEMS agreed to pay Seltaeb $90,000 with Epstein paying his own legal costs of $85,000.

(Right) Dubbed the 'authentic autographed Beatles phonograph', only 5,000 of these Grundig record players were made. They were sold exclusively through the US store chain Gimbels for $29.99.

Paul McCartney's Aston Martin

Baby you can drive my car

Over the years the Beatles, not surprisingly, got through a good few motor cars. As money became more plentiful – and they become more famous – the four of them were all attracted to a wide range of shiny new automobiles that were as important to a group of successful and fashionable young men as the latest in sixties clothing.

As their records sold by the millions and live concerts attracted sell-out audiences, the fab four were able to move on from the cars they owned in Liverpool – such as Ringo Starr's Ford Zephyr and George Harrison's Ford Anglia – to more expensive showroom models. John Lennon was the last Beatle to pass his driving test and actually bought a Ferrari as his first ever car before assembling a collection of at least three Mercedes to go with his hand-painted Rolls–Royce and the rather more sedate Austin Maxi that he seemed to enjoy so much. Starr owned both a customized Radford Mini Cooper and a Mercedes alongside his classic French-made Facel Vega sports car.

Harrison's love of motor cars has been well reported and he graduated to a Jaguar and the coolest sixties car of them all – the Mini Cooper S – before opting for the equally hip E-Type Jaguar. His love of motor racing led him to add an Aston Martin DB5 and a Ferrari 365 to his collection and he was pictured at the wheel of his McLaren FI road car – the fastest production car in the world that retailed at around $1million.

One of Paul McCartney's earliest cars was also a special customized Radford Mini Cooper and he has owned a sizeable and varied selection of autos over the years including a 'hot rod' 1950s Ford Anglia and a Ford Bronco. As man who owns a farm in a remote part of west Scotland, McCartney unsurprisingly added a Land Rover to his collection alongside an Aston Martin DB5 and a Lamborghini 400GT.

He reportedly purchased his dark blue Aston Martin DB6 – with the number plate 64 MAC – in 1964 just after the band had completed filming *A Hard Day's Night* in May and ahead of them setting off on a world tour in June. It came with black leather interior, a radio and a record player and McCartney notched up over 40,000 miles in the classic car before apparently selling it in 1970.

Thirty-two years later the DB5 – the car driven by spy James Bond - came up for auction in London in October 2012 and was sold for over £300,000 at a classic-car sale held in Battersea Park.

In recent years McCartney, an enthusiastic supporter of the environment, has taken ownership of a luxury Hyrbid Lexus worth over £80,000 but there is one important Beatles' car that was never actually owned by any individual group member. In 1966 the company Beatles Ltd. acquired a 1965 Austin Vanden Plas Princess as the group's limousine of choice during the height of Beatlemania. It was used to take them to both private and public events and even made an appearance in the film *Magical Mystery Tour* before it was sold sometime in 1967.

(Right) An appropriate customized number plate for Paul McCartney's Aston Martin, which he bought in 1964 and sold in 1970.

Ticket to the Hollywood Bowl
Sell-out shows

Before 1964 the nearest thing to a pop concert ever held at Los Angeles' prestigious Hollywood Bowl venue was a show on August 24, 1958 which starred the singer and actor Bobby Darin. Almost exactly six years later – on August 23 – the Beatles became the first rock 'n' roll act to play at the Bowl.

On August 19, 1964 they opened their first official US tour with a show at the Cow Palace in San Francisco and, after three shows in Las Vegas, Seattle and Vancouver, they arrived in Los Angeles for a single performance at the celebrated home of the Los Angeles Philharmonic Orchestra.

Opened in 1922, the Hollywood Bowl was the largest natural amphitheatre in the US with a capacity of over 18,000. It boasts a famous shell like arch over the stage area which was conceived by the architect Frank Lloyd Wright who built the original shell for the venue's 1927 and 1928 seasons.

Tickets for the Beatles show – one of 26 dates during their month long tour of the US – went on sale four months in advance and sold out in less than three and a half hours. The group's producer George Martin also chose the Bowl as the venue for the first official live recording of the Beatles. "I thought we should record the Hollywood Bowl concert and I arranged for Capitol to provide their engineers." However, he had underestimated the impact the fans would have on his recording. "It was one continual screaming sound and it was very difficult to get a good recording. It was like putting a microphone at the tail of a 747 jet."

The Beatles took to the stage at 9.30pm and played 12 songs during a 35-minute set which was taped for 'future release' and Lennon later explained, "It was the one we enjoyed the most. We got on, and it was big stage, and it was great. We could be heard in a place like the Hollywood Bowl even though the crowd was wild: good acoustics", and Starr was equally impressed to be playing in the Hollywood Bowl. "The shell around the stage was great. It was the Hollywood Bowl – they were impressive places to me. I fell in love with Hollywood then."

The Beatles returned to the Hollywood Bowl in August 1965 and once again both shows were recorded by Capitol Records although it would be a further 12 years before the album of *The Beatles At Hollywood Bowl* was finally released.

When it came out in May 1977, the album compilation contained six tracks – 'Things We Said Today', 'Roll Over Beethoven', 'Boys', 'All My Loving', 'She Loves You' and 'Long Tall Sally' – from the Beatles debut concert at the Hollywood Bowl. A further seven tracks – 'Twist And Shout', 'She's A Woman', 'Dizzy Miss Lizzy', 'Ticket To Ride', 'Can't Buy Me Love', 'Help' and 'A Hard Day's Night' – came from their 1965 concerts and the album, which involved George Martin remixing and enhancing the original tapes, reached number one in the UK and peaked at number two in the US.

(Above) The Beatles on stage during their debut appearance at the Hollywood Bowl in 1964.

(Right) Tickets for the Beatles only show at the Hollywood Bowl in 1964.

(Overleaf) The illuminated 'sold out' sign for the Beatles' appearances at the Hollywood Bowl in 1964 and 1965.

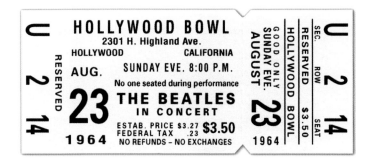

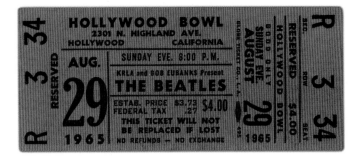

Grammy award for 'A Hard Day's Night'

Winners seven times over

Just two days after the Beatles performed at their third NME Poll Winners concert in London on April 11, 1965, they were being honoured at an even more prestigious awards event in America. The 'Fab Four' had finally made it on to the list of nominees for a Grammy.

First awarded in 1959 for "musical accomplishments", the Grammys were introduced by the National Academy of Recording Arts & Sciences (NARAS) and named in honour of the gramophone invented by Emile Berliner.

The Beatles initial recognition by America's most important music awards came with four nominations which reflected their achievements in America in 1964. Their first US number one single 'I Want To Hold Your Hand' earned them a nomination for Record of the Year while 'A Hard Day's Night' was among the contenders for Best Contemporary Song. They were also named as Best New Artist and 'A Hard Day's Night' was nominated as Best Performance by a Vocal Group.

The song 'A Hard Day's Night' was the hastily created title track from the Beatles debut film which they had to come up with once it was decided that it would be the title of the movie. "This wasn't usually the way we worked because we didn't write songs to order," explained McCartney after he and Lennon had been charged with creating the new composition. "We thought about it and

it seemed a bit ridiculous writing a song called 'A Hard Day's Night' – it sounded funny at the time."

And by mid-April 1964 they were ready to record their new effort in Abbey Road Studios. In nine takes done in a single session between 10am and 1pm on April 16, the Beatles finished the song with producer George Martin, who played piano on the track, explaining "We knew it would open both the film and the soundtrack LP so we wanted a particularly strong and effective beginning. The strident guitar chord was a perfect launch."

At the ceremony in Los Angeles the Beatles lost out to Stan Getz and Astrid Gilberto and 'The Girl From Ipanema' as Record of the Year and were beaten by 'Hello Dolly' in the Best Song category. However, they held off fellow Brit Petula Clark to win the title Best New Artist while 'A Hard Day's Night' won Best Performance by a Group ahead of America's premier folk trio Peter Paul and Mary.

After their initial Grammy success the Beatles went on to win a further six awards – *Sgt Pepper's Lonely Hearts Club Band* won Best Album and Best Contemporary Album in 1968, *Let It Be* was Best Original Score in 1979, *The Beatles Anthology* was Best Long Form Music Video in 1996 and in 1997 'Free As A Bird' was named Best Pop Performance by a Group – and they were also awarded the Grammy Trustees Award in 1972.

(Right) The Beatles' first US Grammy success was for 'A Hard Day's Night', which was one of the four nominations they received at the 1964 awards show.

NATIONAL ACADEMY OF RECORDING ARTS & SCIENCES
THE BEATLES
BEST PERFORMANCE BY A VOCAL GROUP
1964
"A HARD DAY'S NIGHT"

John Lennon's Ivor Novello award

Honouring the writers

The Ivor Novello Awards were instituted by the British Academy of Songwriters, Composers and Authors (BASCA) in 1955 to honour excellence in British music writing, and in the 1960s there were no better song writers in the UK pop music business than the Beatles' John Lennon and Paul McCartney.

Considered to be a "prestigious" award, the 'Ivors' recognized the achievements of the composers rather than performers and the Beatles joined a long list of prestigious winners including Joe Meek, Cat Stevens, Pete Townshend, the Gibb Brothers, Elton John and David Bowie.

They earned their first awards in October 1964 – when the album *A Hard Day's Night* was mid-way through its five-month residency at the top of the UK chart – for a song released in 1963. She Loves You was recognized as both The Best Selling Song and as The Most Broadcast/Performed Work and as an added bonus the Beatles' 'I Want To Hold Your Hand' was the second Best Selling Record and 'All My Loving' was the second Most Outstanding Song.

At the same ceremony all four Beatles plus their manager Brian Epstein and producer George Martin were presented with a Special Award for Outstanding Services to British Music.

With their first awards under their belts the Beatles were rewarded again in 1965 when Can't Buy Me Love was named as both the Best Selling Record and the Most Broadcast/Performed Work. This time McCartney turned up at the awards ceremony held at London's Savoy Hotel on July 13, 1965 to collect the prizes and also to hear 'A Hard Day's Night' named as the second Most Performed Work and also runner-up in the Outstanding Theme From a Radio/TV or Film while 'I Feel Fine' took second place as Best Selling Record.

McCartney's 1965 song 'Yesterday', which even though he created it as a solo composition was credited to Lennon/McCartney, took the 'Ivor' in 1966 as Outstanding Song of the Year while 'We Can Work It Out' was named Best Selling Record ahead of 'Help!'

The Beatles were again to the fore at the 1967 awards when their earlier works 'Michelle' and 'Yellow Submarine' were named as Most Performed Work and Best Selling Record in 1966 respectively. This meant that the Beatles had notched up a record four successive 'Ivor' awards for the UK's Best Selling Record.

In 1968 the song 'She's Leaving Home', from the Beatles' 1967 album *Sgt Pepper's Lonely Hearts Club Band*, was named Best British Song while McCartney also collected a solo 'Ivor' when 'Love In the Open Air' – from his debut soundtrack for the film *The Family Way* – was voted Best Instrumental. The Beatles track 'Hello Goodbye' was named as the second Best Selling Record of the Year.

The following year the Beatles once again earned the Best Selling Single Award for 'Hey Jude' and they followed up with their sixth Best Selling Single title in 1970 for the 1969 song 'Get Back'. The 1970 'Ivor' awards also saw the group win the title for Most Requested Song On Radio with 'Ob-La-Di, Ob-La-Da'.

The Beatles' final Ivor Novello Awards – they were named in tribute to the Welsh-born composer and performer who died in 1951 – came in the form of individual prizes to the group's two major song writers. In 1980 McCartney was awarded a Special Ivor Novello Award for International Achievement and in 1989 he received an award for his Outstanding Contribution to British Music – eight years after Lennon had been recognized with the same award just three months after his death in 1980.

(Right) John Lennon's 1968 'Ivor' for 'She's Leaving Home' – which he shared with co-composer Paul McCartney – was one of 17 Ivor Novello awards won by the members of the Beatles.

Unpublished photo collection

From Cavendish Avenue, London NW8

While his fellow Beatles all took the advice of their accountants and invested in sizeable and expensive properties outside London, Paul McCartney resisted the urge to leave town and move to the country.

After living in the Wimpole Street house of his girlfriend Jane Asher's parents, McCartney opted to buy a three-storey Georgian town house for the two of them and in April 1965 he paid £40,000 for number 7, Cavendish Avenue in St John's Wood, close to Lords cricket ground and Abbey Road Studios. After extensive renovations and refurbishing – costing a reported £20,000 – McCartney moved in to the house in March 1966.

"When I moved it was to St John's Wood, but it was in the middle of London," McCartney explained. "I was still enthralled with London. I loved the sense of history and so I was eager to stay there, to be near the theatre, to be near everything."

As it was close to EMI's studios, the house also became a base for the other Beatles during their recording sessions and with the addition of a top-floor music room, McCartney was able to work on new songs in the privacy of his town house and 'Penny Lane', 'Getting Better' and 'Hey Jude' were all part-created in Cavendish Avenue.

The house was often besieged by fans who regularly took their own photographs of McCartney as he came and went. Indeed, it seems that the song 'She Came In Through The Bathroom Window' may have been inspired by some of the Apple Scruffs – a dedicated group of Beatles' fans – who broke into McCartney's house by using a ladder to get through the bathroom window.

McCartney held meetings in his house – including discussing the cover to the *Sgt Pepper* album cover with designer Peter Black and EMI issues with the company's chairman Sir Joseph Lockwood – and also entertained, among others, art dealer Robert Fraser, artist Andy Warhol and members of the Monkees. The latter went from the Cavendish Avenue house to Abbey Road Studios for the February 10, 1967 recording of 'A Day in The Life'.

The house was also the venue for meetings between McCartney and Rolling Stone Mick Jagger, who lived in nearby Marylebone Road with his girlfriend, Marianne Faithfull. She who once recalled, "We would go and see them a lot, but I don't remember him coming to us. Mick always had to come to his house because he was Paul McCartney, you went to him." While the Beatle also believes he turned Jagger on to pot in the music room of his house – "which is funny because everyone would have thought it would have been the other way round" – the two musicians also met in Cavendish Avenue to compare schedules, in order to make sure that the Beatles and the Rolling Stones didn't clash with single releases.

Over the years McCartney has brought into his house paintings by Magritte and Peter Blake plus sculptures by Takis and Eduardo Paolozz, in addition to a circular bed reputedly given to him by Groucho Marx. He also created a meditation space in the garden where over the years a variety of animals – including chickens and at least one goat – have also found a home.

Even though McCartney rarely lives in the house in Cavendish Avenue – he has other properties in Scotland, Sussex and America – he has never sold the London base he created opposite the home of fellow Liverpool singer Billy Fury.

(Right) Photographs taken by Beatles' fans who waited in Cavendish Avenue, St John's Wood, London, to get a picture of Paul McCartney outside his house.

John Lennon's Rolls–Royce

A hippy car with all mod cons

A few years back, when reflecting on his father's skill as a driver and his choice of cars, Julian Lennon said, "Despite Dad being the worst driver ever he certainly had a few unforgettable cars like the psychedelic Rolls-Royce."

In fact Lennon's first born son was just two years old when the 24-year-old Beatle took ownership of the Rolls-Royce Phantom V – with the license number FJB 111C – in June 1965. Made at the Rolls-Royce factory in Crewe, it was originally finished in standard Valentine Black, weighed three tons and went alongside Lennon's Austin Maxi and stretch Mercedes which he also drove despite his notoriously poor eyesight.

After a year Lennon, who installed a radio telephone (number Weybridge 46676) in December 1965, added a rear seat which converted into a double bed, a custom made sound system (with an exterior loud hailer), a television and a refrigerator. And in the first two years in which he owned it, Lennon's luxury car travelled just over 29,000 miles which included the vehicle – plus a chauffeur – being transported to Spain where he was filming *How I Won The War*.

By that time Lennon had tired of the car's traditional matt black finish and he approached the coachworks company J P Fallon in Chertsey, Surrey to help with the idea of re-spraying the car with a psychedelic pattern. They hired local artist Steve Weaver who created a design of flowers and scrolls which he painted on to the car in an exercise costing a total of £2,000.

The car was transformed into a major talking point and even brought an angry reaction from purists who were offended by Lennon's decision to 'deface' a Rolls-Royce. When Lennon and Ono moved to New York in 1970, the Rolls-Royce was shipped to the US where it was borrowed by a host of rock stars – including the Rolling Stones and Bob Dylan – until Lennon, having decided not to sell it, put the car in storage.

In 1977, following a deal with the US Internal Revenue, Lennon donated the car to a division of the famous Smithsonian Institute in return for a major tax credit and it was eventually put on display for three months in October 1978 at the Cooper-Hewitt Museum in New York. In 1985 the Museum decided to auction the Rolls-Royce through Sotheby's who estimated it would fetch between $200,000 and $300,000. In fact Ripley International, the owners of Ripley's *Believe It or Not!* TV show and museum, paid $2,299,000 for the car which they loaned to the Expo '86 exhibition in Vancouver and eventually ownership was transferred from Ripley International to the company's Canadian owner Jim Pattison, who has been ranked as Canada's third richest man.

Pattison in turn presented the car as a gift to British Columbia, and the Phantom V was put on display in the province's Transportation Museum before being moved to the Royal British Columbia Museum in Victoria, where it has been displayed and occasionally used to help with fund raising.

(Right) The psychedelic Rolls-Royce bought by John Lennon in 1965 and re-painted at a cost of £2,000 two years later.

Shea Stadium poster

"The most exciting thing we've ever done"

Almost a year after they had set out on their first tour of America, the Beatles returned to the States to open an 11-date trip across the States in the vast open-air stadium that was home to the New York Mets baseball team.

Shea Stadium in the Queens district of New York was filled with over 55,000 fans when the Beatles played there on August 15, 1965. "Shea Stadium was an enormous place," said Harrison. "It was the first time that one of those stadiums had been used for a rock concert." And he was right as the closest thing had been a fund raiser played by Sammy Davis Jr in front of just of 2,000 people.

The Shea Stadium event was the brainchild of American promoter Sid Bernstein who had to pay all the staging and security costs (plus insurance of £25,000 to Lloyds of London) for the show which also featured fellow Brits Sounds Incorporate alongside Brenda Holloway and the King Curtis Band. The Beatles travelled by limousine from their hotel in Manhattan to the heliport where they took a helicopter, which landed them on the roof of the nearby World Fair's building. From there they were driven to the final 100 yards to the venue in a Wells Fargo security truck.

The Beatles were introduced by disc jockey Murray the K and their ten-song set was filmed by TV host Ed Sullivan's production company – in association with the Beatles and manager Epstein – for a 50 minute television special which was eventually shown by the BBC in March 1966.

Drowned out by screams throughout their show – despite Vox supplying special 100-watt amplifiers – the Beatles, wearing khaki semi-military jackets, were still mightily impressed with the event. "It was marvellous," said Lennon. "It was the biggest crowd we had ever played to anywhere in the world. It was the biggest live show anybody's ever done, they told us. And it was fantastic, the most exciting thing we've ever done."

Not only was it "exciting" and "fantastic", it was also highly profitable as the Beatles' share of the world record takings of £304,000 amounted to a record $160,000.

A year after their debut show in the Shea Stadium, the Beatles returned to the New York venue on August 23, 1966 as part of their final live tour. Although the venue failed to sell out – there were 11,000 seats unsold – the group still took home new world record takings of $189,000 from the gross income of $292,000 but the unsold seats had a more serious impact on the Beatles touring plans according to producer George Martin. "... it was against this background that they said, 'Right, we definitely won't do any more.'"

(Above) A commemorative key ring produced by promoter Sid Bernstein when the Beatles played Shea Stadium in New York.

(Right) This poster advertised the Beatles' second appearance at Shea Stadium in 1966 – six days before that last ever concert.

SID BERNSTEIN
PRESENTS THE
BEATLES
IN PERSON

PLUS ALL STAR SHOW

SHEA STADIUM
AUG. 23 - 1966 7:30 P.M.

All Seats Reserved: $4.50, 5.00, 5.75 - phone 265-2280 For Information

TICKETS NOW AT

SINGER SHOP RECORD DEPT. Rockefeller Center Promenade, 49th - 50th Streets on Fifth Avenue

1965 US Tour personalized luggage tags

Back in the USA

Almost exactly a year on from their first major tour of America, the Beatles returned to play a second series of concerts in the country that was the world's largest music market and a place where they reigned supreme.

When they arrived in New York for their record-breaking opening show at Shea Stadium on August 15, 1965, the group were on the verge of notching up their ninth US number-one single with the release of 'Help!' while the album of the same name was about to join the list as the Beatles' sixth American chart topper.

From New York the Beatles flew on to Toronto where their two shows at Maple Leaf Gardens on August 17 were watched by over 18,000 fans while 30,000 crammed into Atlanta's Stadium the next night to see a single show. On the next four nights the Beatles played seven shows in Houston, Chicago, Minneapolis and Portland to more than 130,000 fans.

After flying to California on August 23 to prepare for their show in San Diego on August 28, the Beatles rested up in Los Angeles before embarking on a historic journey across LA on August 27 to meet Elvis Presley in his Bel Air mansion in Perugia Way. The meeting, which followed Paul McCartney talking to the King on the telephone back in August 1964 and was instigated by Presley's manager Col. Tom Parker, resulted in the fab four and Elvis performing 'You're My World' during a brief and unrecorded jam session.

Following their San Diego show, the Beatles played two shows at the Hollywood Bowl on August 29 and August 30 which, in addition to earning them gate receipts of over $90,000, were recorded and later formed a large part of the *The Beatles At The Hollywood Bowl* album.

The tenth and final concert in their 16-day trip to the US took place at San Francisco's Cow Palace on August 31 when over 18,000 fans saw two shows at the venue where the band had opened their first tour year earlier.

(Right) The Beatles were given these individual luggage tags when they flew with Trans World Airlines to America for their 16-day tour in 1965.

(Overleaf) The Beatles on the makeshift stage at the White Sox Stadium in Chicago, which was specially built for their two shows on August 20, 1965.

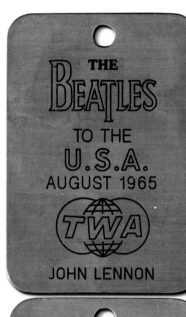

MBE medals
A badge from the Queen

No pop music star – not even Cliff Richard – had been honoured with an award from royalty until the Beatles were named as MBEs in Queen Elizabeth II's Birthday Honours List on June 12, 1965.

It was Prime Minister (and Liverpool MP) Harold Wilson who recommended the Beatles for their award as Members of the British Empire but when the news broke protests poured into Buckingham Palace from existing medal holders. A retired colonel returned 12 medals while former Canadian MP Hector Dupuis complained, "The British house of royalty has put me on the same level as a bunch of vulgar numbskulls."

At the same time the Beatles had mixed reactions to the news. "There are two ways to look at it," said McCartney. "Either it's a great honour that's being bestowed on you – and I think to some degree we did believe that – or (if you want to be cynical) it's a very cheap way to reward people."

And while Starr said, "We're going to meet the Queen and she's going to give us a badge. I thought 'This is cool'", it seems that Lennon was less impressed.

After he had ignored the original letter from Buckingham Palace asking if he would accept an honour, he eventually agreed to accept the medal. "He [Brian Epstein] and a few other people persuaded me that it was in our interest to take it" although he later added, "We had to do a lot of selling out then. Taking the MBE was a sell-out for me."

It wasn't until October 26, 1965 that the Beatles, who were engrossed in recording sessions for their *Rubber Soul* album, finally went to Buckingham Palace to collect their medals from the Queen. Manager Epstein did not go to the Palace with the group as he was not nominated although Princess Margaret was quoted as saying, "I think the Beatles believe that MBE stands for Mister Brian Epstein."

During the ceremony, the Queen asked Starr how long the group had been together and he and McCartney quipped, "We've been together now for forty years and it don't seem a day too much" while the stories of them smoking a joint in the Palace toilets may have been exaggerated. "We never smoked marijuana at the investiture", said Harrison who then explained that the group did go to the toilet as they were nervous. "And in there we smoked a cigarette. Years later I'm sure John was thinking back and remembering 'Oh yes, we went in the toilet and smoked' and that turned into a reefer."

Four years later – on November 25, 1969 – Lennon decided to return his MBE to The Queen as a protest against wars in Nigeria and Vietnam and his latest record dropping down the hit parade. In a note on Bag Productions headed notepaper, sent from Apple's offices at 3 Savile Row, he said, "Your Majesty, I am returning this MBE in protest against Britain's involvement in the Nigeria-Biafra thing, against our support of America in Vietnam and against 'Cold Turkey' slipping down the charts." And he signed it – "with love John Lennon".

In 2009 the MBE which Lennon returned was discovered in a royal vault at the Chancery Department of the Royal Household together with the Beatles' letter of protest. While fans requested that the medal – which was described as "a vital piece of Beatles memorabilia" – should be put on display, preferably in Liverpool, a spokesman for Buckingham Palace explained that they would automatically return the medal to the original recipient on request during his lifetime and added, "The Central Chancery would therefore only consider releasing insignia if they had a direct approach from the recipient's legal next of kin."

(Right) An MBE medal like those awarded to the Beatles in 1965. John Lennon returned his medal in 1969 and it was discovered in a royal vault ten years later.

Help! script

Roll the cameras – again

In February 1965, the Beatles began work on their second film, which featured a script written by American Marc Behm, who had written the movie *Charade*, and Englishman Charles Wood, who had worked with director Dick Lester on the film *The Knack*.

Shooting of *Help!* began in Nassau, the capital of the Bahamas, on February 24, two days after the cast and a crew comprising more than 70 people had arrived on the Caribbean islands, where the temperature was in the nineties. As the filming was set to move on to Austria in less than a month's time, it was imperative that none of the Beatles got any sort of a suntan, as the scenes in Europe were set to feature first in the final film.

For the March shooting in Austria, the Beatles were each given a special wardrobe of black trousers and assorted black tops plus black sealskin ski boots. The film, which featured a cast including established actors Leo McKern, Eleanor Bron, Warren Mitchell and Dandy Nichols plus roadie Mal Evans, was completed in May 1965 after extra scenes had been shot around London, on Salisbury Plain and in Twickenham Studios. *Help!*, which was briefly titled *Beatles Two* and *Eight Arms To Hold You*, was once again produced by Walter Shenson and cost a total of $1.5 million to complete.

The film's premier was held at the London Pavilion cinema on July 29, with Princess Margaret and Lord Snowdon attending the screening, which was sponsored by the Variety Club of Great Britain in aid of the Docklands Settlement and the Variety Club's own Heart Fund. Two weeks later *Help!* opened in America and in September it won first prize at the Rio de Janeiro International Film Festival.

While producer Shenson described *Help!* as "a holiday picture" and then explained, "It was filmed in two totally contrasting holiday resorts. We travelled from calypso to yodel with a lot of yeah yeah thrown in", one reviewer commented, "These boys are the closest thing to the Marx Brothers since The Marx Brothers." Despite distributors United Artists, Shenson and Lester all being keen on the idea of making another Beatles feature film, a third movie never materialized.

The soundtrack album from *Help!* reached number one in the UK – the group's fifth successive chart topper – and, as with *A Hard Day's Night*, only one side actually featured songs from the film.

(Above) An early script book for the Beatles' second film, when it was simply entitled *Beatles Two*.

(Right) The Beatles assemble in the snow in Austria, in March 1964, to shoot scenes for the re-titled film, *Help!*

Abbey Road piano

The battered upright 'jangle piano'

From June 6, 1962 – the first day the Beatles set foot in Abbey Road – through to August 1969, EMI's famous recording studio in north London was at the very heart of the group's creativity. By the time all four group members assembled together in the studio for the very last time, the Beatles had recorded twelve albums and 22 singles – and all but one of the albums had been made in Abbey Road.

McCartney also noted that in the early days they were not allowed in all areas of the studio. "We weren't even allowed into the control room then. It was Us and Them. They had white shirts and ties in the control rooms, they were the grown ups. That was how it stayed until we were very famous."

While most of the Beatles' recording time was spent in studio two, they did use the much larger studio one on occasion. It was there that they played 'All You Need Is Love' and were filmed for the BBC's *Our World* global broadcast – and also studio three, the smallest room at Abbey Road, which was originally used for solo classical piano recordings.

When the Beatles did eventually go into studio three, one of the things they found was a slightly battered upright piano made by the London firm of Challen who supplied pianos to the BBC before adding EMI to their list if clients. In fact during the group's first recording session in studio three on April 6, 1966, they recorded a track which had the working title 'Mark I' and would eventually become the revolutionary creation known as 'Tomorrow Never Knows'. On April 6 – and on the following day – the Challen piano was used alongside an organ and the Beatles regular guitar, bass and drums to create what producer George Martin described as "a great innovation" as everything was fed through a revolving Leslie speaker housed in a Hammond organ.

The same keyboard – known as a 'jangle piano' – was used on the group's June 1966 number one hit single 'Paperback Writer' and on later recordings of 'Ob-La-Di, Ob-La-Da' and 'Old Brown Shoe' while a second Challen piano in studio two was used as part of the extraordinary almost one-minute long E major chord played simultaneously on three pianos by John Lennon, Paul McCartney, Ringo Starr and road manager Mal Evans on February 22, 1967 which became the ending to the song 'A Day In The Life'.

The Challen from studio three – which Pink Floyd, it is claimed, used during recordings of their albums *The Dark Side Of The Moon* and *Wish You Were Here* – turned up in a London auction in 2010 when it was expected to sell for around £150,000. It was withdrawn from the sale following objections by EMI/Abbey Road who reclaimed ownership of the instrument. The appearance of the piano in the sale alerted the studios to the fact that they actually had two Challen pianos – one from the late 1950s and the other from the early 1960s – which were used by the Beatles.

(Right) One of the two Challen pianos in Abbey Road, which the Beatles used in studio three on 'Tomorrow Never Knows' and 'Paperback Writer'.

Yesterday and Today album cover

Complaints over the 'butcher cover'

Over the years Capitol Records in America managed to upset the Beatles, their manager and producer by altering both the track listing and the cover design of albums in an effort to meet the never-ending demand for more and more recordings from the group.

In June 1966 they came up with their sixth US-only compilation album which was made up of tracks from the original UK versions of *Help!*, *Rubber Soul* and *Revolver* which were left off the US versions. Created to take advantage of the success of the US-only single release 'Yesterday' – a number one for four weeks in 1965 – they decided to title the new album *Yesterday ... and Today*.

As they also had to create new artwork for the cover, Capitol chose to use a photograph taken in London by Robert Whitaker, which had been used in the press as an advert for the group's single release 'Paperback Writer' and had also appeared on the front cover of the music paper *Disc* in June 1966. It featured the four band members wearing white 'lab-coats' and holding pieces of meat and the bodies and heads of baby dolls.

Recalling the London session Lennon said, "The photographer was a bit of a surrealist and he brought along these babies and pieces of meat and doctor's coats, so we really got into it." On the other hand Harrison recounted, "I thought it was gross and I also thought it was stupid" while McCartney explained, "It didn't seem too offensive to us. It was just dolls and a lot of meat. I don't know really what he was trying to say but it seemed a little more original than the things the rest of the people were getting us to do."

It seems that when it came to the idea of using the shot as the cover for an album, it was Lennon who was the prime mover. "I especially pushed for it to be an album cover, just to break the image" was his thinking and the President of Capitol was it seems, behind him all the way when he said. "The original cover, created in England, was intended to be 'pop art' satire."

Unfortunately American record dealers, media and even fans of the group did not like what they saw as the first advance copies of the album were issued. Capitol was flooded with complaints at what was dubbed 'the butcher cover' and they immediately withdrew the record which meant that, at a total cost of over $200,000, a new cover had to be pasted on the front of more than 500,000 albums while a mountain of advertising material had to be destroyed.

The replacement cover – which showed Lennon, Harrison and Starr gathered around a steamer trunk that McCartney was sitting in – was also taken by Whitaker although the original purple background was airbrushed white in order to allow Capitol to drop in the lettering from the original album. According to Lennon "... there was some kind of fuss, as usual, and they were all sent back in or withdrawn and they stuck that awful looking picture of us looking just as deadbeat but supposed to be a happy-go-lucky foursome."

And while the album *Yesterday ... and Today* went to number one in America – replacing Frank Sinatra's *Strangers in the Night* – on July 30, 1966 and remained there for five weeks (until it was succeeded by *Revolver*) it is the original 'banned' cover that remains in high demand, with original sealed copies fetching over $35,000.

(Right) Images of the infamous 'butcher cover' from the *Yesterday ... And Today* album (right), and the replacement cover shot – both of which were taken by British photographer Robert Whittaker.

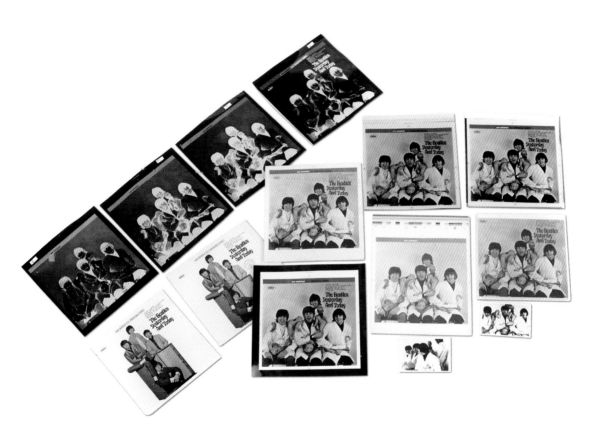

Candlestick Park ticket

The final curtain

We'd done about 1400 shows and I certainly felt that was it" was how George Harrison summed up the situation as the Beatles brought their touring career to an end exactly seven years to the day after they had opened the Casbah Club in Liverpool in 1959.

As they began their third tour of America in Chicago in August 1966, it was also clear to Starr that the constant round of live concerts and endless tours had lost its appeal. "In the end no one enjoyed touring. We've had enough of performing for ever."

After playing 19 shows across America, the Beatles arrived in San Francisco on August 29 to play to 25,000 fans – who paid an average of $5 a ticket – in Candlestick Park on a bill where they were supported by the Cyrkle, the Ronettes and Bobby Hebb. They were introduced by local disc jockey Gene Nelson and went into an 11 song set which began with Chuck Berry's 'Rock And Roll Music' and closed with Little Richard's 'Long Tall Sally'.

One of the main reasons the Beatles gave up on touring was the reaction of the fans who made so much noise that the group could not hear themselves play. "It had been four years of legging around in a screaming mania" said Harrison while Lennon suggested, "I reckon we could send out four waxwork dummies of ourselves and that would satisfy the crowds. Beatles concerts are nothing to do with music anymore."

While manager Epstein missed the last show his group ever played following the theft of cash and documents from his hotel room in Los Angeles, press officer Tony Barrow was around with his trusty Philips tape recorder when McCartney said, "Make me a recording of tonight's final concert will you?" even though nobody had talked of the show as being the final appearance by the Beatles. "None of the boys had ever asked me to record souvenir tapes of concerts before", says Barrow who asked himself, "Was he [Paul] resigned to the fact that San Francisco was the end of the road?"

Barrow made a single copy of the concert cassette for himself – "I kept it under lock and key in a drawer of my office desk" – and gave the original to McCartney, but years later a recording of the show re-appeared as a bootleg album. And the Beatles' former press office was left to conclude, "If you hear a bootleg version of the final concert that finishes during 'Long Tall Sally', it must have come either from Paul's copy or mine, but we never did identify the music thief!"

In fact McCartney was the last of the group to be persuaded that the Beatles' days as a live touring band were over, but finally he agreed that "it had started to become less enjoyable", particularly as they were no longer playing to sell-out crowds; surprisingly there were 20,000 empty seats in Candlestick Park. McCartney concluded, "The quality of the music wasn't good and it wasn't getting any better with the touring. We all agreed that maybe going into recording would be the new thing to turn us all on."

After their final show, the Beatles flew back to Los Angeles and the house they had rented in Beverly Hills. It was on the plane journey that Harrison announced, "Well, that's it. I'm not a Beatle anymore."

(Above) A $4.50 ticket to see the Beatles give their final concert performance in San Francisco from the upper stand.

(Right) The poster advertising the Beatles last ever show at Candlestick Park on Monday, August 29, 1966.

'Strawberry Fields' shoot list

Childhood memories

'Strawberry Fields Forever' – with its companion A-side 'Penny Lane' – was arguably one of the greatest records the Beatles ever released. It was without question the best Beatles' single never to reach number one in the UK charts and it remained one of Lennon's favourite songs.

Growing up in Menlove Avenue in Liverpool with his Aunt Mimi, Lennon would crawl through the hedge to play in the grounds of the nearby Strawberry Field children's orphanage, where he also attended garden fetes with his auntie.

Located in Beaconsfield Road, Woolton, the house Strawberry Field, which so inspired Lennon, was built in around 1870 and bought by the Salvation Army in 1934 for use as an orphanage. It was eventually demolished in the 1970s when a smaller purpose-built children's home was created with a unit called Lennon Court. The home was finally closed in 2005, although the original gates to Strawberry Field, which were painted bright red, remained in place until 2010 when a new set were erected.

Lennon had composed the song while on location in Spain to film his part in *How I Won The War* and at the studio in his Kenwood home before returning to Abbey Road Studios, after nearly five months absence, in November 1966. Recalling that they were now off the road permanently and back in the studio with a collection of new songs, McCartney said, "Strawberry Fields is the song that John had about the old Salvation Army home for kids he used to live next door to in Liverpool. We related it to youth, golden summers and fields of strawberry. I knew what he was talking about."

The Beatles worked on Lennon's song during seven separate sessions spread over more than three weeks. As the song took shape it became apparent that there were two distinct versions – a basic group version and a fuller effort involving trumpets and strings which had been scored by producer George Martin, who recalled that Lennon had told him, "I like it but it's worked out much harder than I thought it would be. I'd like you to do a score and maybe use a few cellos and a bit of brass."

Finally, on December 22, 1966, Lennon decided that he liked both versions and asked Martin to "join the beginning of the first one to the end of the second one." The completed version, with the join reported to be after 60 seconds from the start, was released together with Penny Lane on February 17, 1967 and, after 11 successive number ones, it became the first Beatles single not to top the official charts since 1963.

It was held off the number one spot by Engelbert Humperdinck's 'Release Me' and while Harrison said, "It was pretty bad, wasn't it, that Engelbert Humperdinck stopped 'Strawberry Fields Forever' getting to number one?", Lennon, confirming that he always read the charts, simply observed, "There's room for everything. I don't mind Engelbert Humperdinck. They're the cats. It's their scene."

(Above) The wrought-iron gates leading to Strawberry Field Children's orphanage, in Liverpool.

(Right) The call sheet for the filming of the video for the Beatles track 'Strawberry Fields Forever', January 1967.

BEATLES CLIP - Filming 30.1.67

DIRECTOR:	PETER GOLDMAN (LAK 2575)
CAMERAMAN	DON LONG (PAD 2881)
PRODUCTION ASST.	GERRY PEARSON (MAI 5134)
LOCATION ASST.	HOWARD ROSS (RIC 5463)
	TONY BRAMWELL (WR 43687)
ARTISTES	THE BEATLES

- -

LOCATION: KNOLE PARK ESTATE,
          SEVENOAKS,
          KENT.

UNIT CALL: At Location by 0900

ARTISTES CALL   At Location by 10.30

LOCATION CONTACT: Mr Mason,
          Knole Park Estate Office,
          (in Knole House)
          Sevenoaks, Kent.
          (Sevenoaks 53006)

7oaks 0732

HOTEL DRESSING ROOM: BLIGH'S HOTEL,
          The High Street,
          Sevenoaks.
          (Sevenoaks 54092)
          Room booked in name of Tony Bramwell

PROP TRANSPORT: J. BARNES & SONS,
          7, River Street,
          E.C.1.
          (TER 2186)
          Props on location for 0900

LOCATION CATERING   FARMCRAFT,
          39, Malden Road,
          New Malden,
          Surrey
          MAL 6533
          (Catering to be at location to
          serve coffee at 1000 hrs.)

PROPS: (all in Prop Van) DOLLY
          Piano
          6 Tymps & stands
          2 ladders (16' extending to 42')
          plus piano dressings etc.

HIRE CAR: Mr Biddulph (SCO 1567)

Collecting: T. Bramwell 0700 at Nems Office
          P. Goldmann 0730 at 65 Pepys Rd.
                  S.W.20.
          H. Ross 0800 at 15, Larkfield Rd.
               Richmond, Sy.

          & proceed to location. Remains
          under direction of Tony Bramwell.

Julian Lennon's drawing

An idea for a song

At the age of just four John Lennon's son Julian used a painting lesson at his Surrey nursery school to create a drawing which would subsequently inspire the Beatles to produce a track on their multi-million selling album *Sgt Pepper's Lonely Hearts Club Band*.

Julian's painting featured his class friend Lucy O'Donnell, and his mother Cynthia Lennon recalls the day he brought it home for his parents to see "John was sitting on the couch opposite me. Dot [the family's housekeeper] brought Julian in and he showed John a picture of his friend Lucy." Lennon also recounted his first sight of the artwork, "My son came in one day with a picture he painted about a school friend of his named Lucy. He had sketched in some stars in the sky and called it 'Lucy in the Sky With Diamonds'. Simple."

Working at his Kenwood home, Lennon later showed the picture to his song-writing partner McCartney. "I went up to John's house in Weybridge. When I arrived they were having a cup of tea and he [John] said 'Look at this great drawing Julian's done. Look at the title.' He showed me a drawing on a piece of school paper of a little girl with lots of stars and right across the top there was written in very neat child handwriting, 'Lucy in the Sky With Diamonds'.

While Lennon was adamant that the finished song contained no drug references, McCartney was equally convinced it was just about a child's drawing. "And we loved it and she was in the sky and it was very trippy to us. So we went upstairs and started writing it. People later thought 'Lucy in the Sky with Diamonds' was LSD, I swear we didn't notice that when it came out." He also confirmed that it was a song that reflected their joint love of Lewis Carroll's work. "We did the whole thing like an *Alice In Wonderland* idea, being on a boat on the river ..."

While Julian was unable to explain the painting other than to say "I have no idea how the phrase 'Lucy In The Sky With Diamonds' came about – shiny things in the sky probably became diamonds when you are just four", he failed to keep hold of the original work. "The original drawing is as far as I know with Dave Gilmour of Pink Floyd and I've tried to get it back. In legal terms I would own copyright on my drawing but aged four I didn't stamp it as my copyright!"

Never released as a single, 'Lucy In the Sky With Diamonds' was one of the three songs Lennon sang when he joined Elton John on stage at Madison Square Garden on November 28, 1974, for what would be his last ever concert appearance.

In 2009 Julian made contact with Lucy O'Donnell, who was by then Mrs Lucy Vorden, when he heard that she was suffering from the incurable disease lupus. After her death later the same year he wrote the song 'Lucy' in her memory and recorded it as a duet with the singer/songwriter James Scot Cook, with 50% of the proceeds from sales going to help with research into the disease lupus. The single was issued with Julian's original nursery school drawing as the cover.

(Right) Julian Lennon was just four years old when he created this drawing at nursery school, showing 'Lucy in the Sky With Diamonds'.

Sgt Pepper's drum

Roll up roll up ...

Just as they predicted the Beatles, in the aftermath of their decision to stop touring, focused their attention on the recording studio and began work on ideas for an album that was destined to change both the look and sound of popular music.

They began creating *Sgt Pepper's Lonely Hearts Club Band* at Abbey Road Studios in December 1966 and continued through until April 1967 – over 700 hours of recording time at a cost of £25,000.

But it all paid off as, following its release in the first week of June 1967 – it was the first Beatles' album to be released simultaneously worldwide and the first to appear in America without any changes to the track listing – it went to number one in America for 15 weeks, while in the UK it hit the top spot on no fewer than four occasions during the eight months between June 1967 and February 1968. In its first week of release in the UK, the album sold over 250,000 copies and within a month it had passed the half million mark, while in America sales passed 2.5 million copies in three months.

While no singles were issued from the album, controversy still surrounded the Beatles' tenth US number one and their eight British chart topper when the BBC banned the track 'A Day In The Life'. This was because they thought it might encourage drug taking, while the song 'Lucy In The Sky With Diamonds' was linked with the drug LSD. Paul's response to the BBC ban was to explain to the press, "We don't care if they ban our song. It might help the LP."

Although *Sgt Pepper* was labelled as the world's first concept album, John was less than convinced about the description. "... it doesn't go anywhere. All my contributions to the album have absolutely nothing to do with this idea of Sgt Pepper and his band, but it works because we said it worked and that's how the album appeared."

But it wasn't just in a musical sense that *Sgt Pepper* was a landmark album – it also broke most of the rules regarding album cover design. It was one of the earliest gatefold sleeves, included a pull-out and set of cut outs – a moustache, a picture card, a set of sergeant's stripes, two badges and a Beatles stand up – and was the first sleeve to feature printed song lyrics.

The cover was designed by artist Peter Blake, who was knighted in 2002, and photographed by Michael Cooper, who died in 1972, and the original idea was based on each of the Beatles listing their 12 favourite heroes from history to feature on the cover. While the final work does not include all the people chosen by the group, it does feature various unknown characters and people chosen by the designers.

(Above) The Russian version of the cover of *Sgt Pepper's Lonely Hearts Club* album.

(Right) The ornate drum on the *Sgt Pepper* album cover was painted by fairground artist Joseph Ephgrave.

'Within You Without You' lyrics

George's 'strange instrument'

According to George Harrison it was during the filming of *Help!* that he first became aware of Indian music. "We were waiting to shoot the scene in the restaurant when the guy gets thrown in the soup and there were a few Indian musicians playing in the background. I remember picking up the sitar and trying to hold it and thinking 'This is a funny sound'."

From there, Harrison's interest was further aroused by people mentioning the name Ravi Shankar to him. "I talked with David Crosby of the Byrds and he mentioned the name. I went and bought a Ravi record; I put it on and it hit a certain spot in me that I can't explain."

"I went and bought a sitar from a little shop at the top of Oxford Street called Indiacraft. It was a real crummy quality one actually but I bought it and mucked about with it a bit," he recalled and in October 1965 the famous instrument made its debut on a pop record during the recording sessions for the album *Rubber Soul*.

On October 12, the Beatles began work on a track called 'This Bird Has Flown' in Abbey Road Studios and it featured Harrison's double-tracked sitar solo. Further work was done nine days later, by which time the song had been re-titled 'Norwegian Wood', and once again the sitar was featured.

Recalling the 'Norwegian Wood' sessions, Harrison explained that things had reached a point where something else was needed. "We would usually start looking through the cupboard to see if we could come up with something ... I picked up the sitar – it was just lying around; I hadn't really figured out what to do with it. It was quite spontaneous; I found the notes that played the lick. It fitted and it worked."

The other Beatles were, it seems, impressed with Harrison's virtuosity on the new instrument. "It was such a mind blower that we had this strange instrument on a record," said Starr, while Lennon recalled asking his fellow Beatle if he thought he would be able to play on the sitar the piece he had written for the song. "He was not sure whether he could play it yet because he hadn't done much on the sitar but he was willing to have a go, as is his wont, and he learnt the bit and dubbed it on after."

After that impromptu use of the sitar on the Beatles' sixth studio album, Harrison's interest in both Indian music and Eastern religion became more intense. At his first meeting with Shankar in June 1966, at the home of a member of the Asian Music Circle, Harrison asked if he could become his student. This involved Shankar visiting Harrison's home and, according to the Liverpool musician, showing him the basics in sitar playing. "How to hold the sitar, how to sit in the correct position, how to wear the pick on your finger and to begin playing."

Further inspired, Harrison flew to India in 1966 and bought a top-quality sitar from a shop in New Delhi. After the group's final concert in San Francisco, he returned to India for further lessons with the master musician, who was born in 1920 and once observed, "George is a wonderful student and it will not be long before he masters the sitar."

Harrison used the sitar on 'Love You To' on the *Revolver* album and perhaps most famously on his song 'Within You Without You' – which Lennon described as "beautiful" – on *Sgt Pepper's Lonely Hearts Club Band*, when he explained, "There were specific things that I had written, like 'Within You Without You', to try and feature the Indian instruments. Harrison was also instrumental in getting Shankar on the bill at the 1967 Monterey Pop Festival, and he helped his teacher organize the concert for Bangladesh which took place in New York in August 1971.

(Right) George Harrison's hand-written sitar chord sequences and (upside down) lyrics for his song 'Within You Without You'.

INTRO   TANPURA

Sarangi | G M P N̲ | Ṡ N̰ | Ṡ N̰ | Ṡ N̰ |

| P N̲ P | M G | M G̰ | M G | S

G M | P N̲ — | | D - G | P R | P M G   (twice)

G M P G | G M D P D | G M P N̲ Ṡ | P N̲ Ṡ G̰ M̰ G̰

M̰ G̰ M̰ — | M̰ G̰ Ṡ N̲ P N̲ P N M | into second verse (same)

'All You Need Is Love' draft lyrics

A song for 400 million

In 1967 the Beatles were chosen to represent the BBC – and presumably Britain – as part of the world's first television satellite link-up and to appear in front of a potential global audience of over 400 million.

Producer George Martin recalled the moment they all heard that the Beatles had been chosen for the programme, which was to be broadcast to 26 countries. "Brian [Epstein] suddenly whirled in and said that we were to represent Britain in a round-the-world-hook-up and we'd got to write a song. It was a challenge."

The group rose to the challenge, with Lennon coming up with a song entitled 'All You Need Is Love', and while Martin believes that Lennon wrote it especially for the show, McCartney is not so sure. "It was John's song mainly; one of those we had around at the time. It fits very well, so it might have been written especially for the show. But I've got a feeling it was just one of John's songs that was coming anyway."

The first recording session for the Our World television programme took place in Olympic Sound Studios, London, on June 14, when an initial backing track was taped and work continued in Abbey Road over four days including June 24 when, on the eve of the actual broadcast, the 13-piece orchestra, under the baton of ex-Manfred Mann member Mike Vickers, was recorded.

The next day the Beatles, producer George Martin, plus guests Mick Jagger, Keith Richards, Brian Jones, Graham Nash, Eric Clapton Keith Moon and Donovan – and the orchestra – assembled in Abbey Road's cavernous number one studio, which was festooned with balloons and banners, to perform and tape the six-minute live performance of 'All You Need Is Love'. "We went round to EMI for the show", recalled McCartney. "We'd done a lot of pre-recording, so we sang live to the backing track. We went in there early to rehearse with the cameras."

The session began at 2pm on June 25 and the Beatles worked their way through ten takes before getting to the final take 58, which was the version that went out around the world. "It seemed a great idea at the time to sing that song while everybody else was showing knitting in Canada or Irish clog dances in Venezuela," suggested Harrison.

Just over a week after the TV broadcast, 'All You Need Is Love' was released on July 7. The song entered the UK chart at number one and stayed there for four weeks. It was released in America ten days later and again went straight to number one in August, if only for one week.

(Above) Paul McCartney's early hand-written lyrics for the verse and chorus to 'All You Need Is Love'.

(Right) A single-side test pressing of 'All You Need Is Love'.

John's bracelets
A moment for meditation

By the time Maharishi Mahesh Yogi came to the attention of the Beatles, he had been travelling the world for nearly a decade teaching his Transcendental Meditation techniques.

It seems that the driver of the bus to Scotland was born in either 1911, 1917 or 1918 – ascetics and monks have a tradition of renouncing family connections and history. He became a disciple of Swami Brahmananda Saraswati, began teaching in the mid-1950s and first travelled to America in 1958. In 1960, as he toured around Europe, he visited Britain and appeared on television and in newspapers and year later he gave a lecture to 5,000 people at London's Royal Albert Hall.

Around the same time he established his first Transcendental Meditation training course in Rishikesh in India but it was in 1967 when he entered the world of the Beatles. George Harrison's wife Pattie Boyd attended a lecture the Maharishi gave at Caxton Hall in London and her enthusiasm, coupled with a series of adverts on London Underground stations, persuaded the Beatles to attend his personal appearance at the London Hilton Hotel on August 24, 1967.

"We wanted to try and expand spiritually or at least find some sort of format for all the various things we were interested in," recounted McCartney ahead of the Beatles paying 7s.6d (37½p) for a ticket to the talk. "We all got tickets and sat down the near the front row. There were lots of flowers on the stage and he came on and sat cross-legged. And he looked great and he talked very well and started to explain."

The Maharishi – dubbed the "giggling guru" by the media – invited the Beatles to join a course he was holding at Normal College in Bangor. Arriving on Friday August 25, 1967, the Beatles had invited manager Brian Epstein to join them in North Wales and he suggested that they would be down after the August Bank Holiday on Monday. The stay in Bangor was "incredible" according to Lennon who added, "The Maharishi reckons the message will get through if we can put it across" before explaining the financial arrangement. "Another groovy thing: everybody gives one week's wages when they join. I think it's the fairest thing I've ever heard of. And that's all you ever pay, just the once."

Tragically, the Beatles stay in Bangor was cut short when they received news that Epstein had been found dead in his London flat on August 27, but six months later in February 1968 they renewed their commitment to the Maharishi by travelling to India for a planned three-month stay at his ashram in Risikesh. However, following Starr's departure after just ten days, McCartney then departed after about a month, although Lennon and Harrison stayed on until an allegation that the Maharishi had acted improperly towards actress Mia Farrow stirred them into leaving.

While Harrison said later that he was convinced nothing happened – "Now historically, there's the story that something went on that shouldn't have done – but nothing did" – the Beatles distanced themselves from the Maharishi who died in 2008. A disillusioned Lennon would say, "We believe in meditation but not the Maharishi and his scene. But that's a personal mistake we made in public", while McCartney added, "We thought there was more to him than there was, but he's human and for a while we thought he wasn't."

Even though he left disappointed, Lennon found some inspiration in India as he wrote 'Dear Prudence' about Mia Farrow's sister and featured the mantra *jai guru dev om* in the song 'Across the Universe', while for legal reasons his song 'Maharishi' was re-written and eventually re-titled Sexy Sadie.

(Right) John Lennon wore these Guru Deva bracelets in India in February 1968, when he studied with Maharishi Mahesh Yogi and meditation teacher Guru Deva.

George Harrison's guitar 'Rocky'

A paint and nail varnish job

In the midst of the summer of love – with psychedelia dominating fashion, music and attitudes – the Beatles could reflect on the success of their *Sgt Pepper's Lonely Hearts Club* album as they prepared for the single and television broadcast of 'All You Need Is Love'. And at the same time Harrison decided to spruce up his Fender Stratocaster guitar with a do-it-yourself paint job.

"I painted it before we did the *All You Need Is Love* TV satellite show. It was powder blue originally," said Harrison before adding, "We were painting everything at that time."

Using day-glo and enamel paint, plus his wife Patti's green nail varnish, Harrison transformed his 1962 Sonic Blue guitar into a piece of psychedelic art. "Colourful clothes, colourful houses and cars, and it was just logical to have a coloured guitar," explained Harrison. Having completed the job, and added the Gene Vincent song title 'Be Bop A Lula', to the body Harrison admitted, "It's not so much a great paint job but that's the way it came out. And the guitar's called Rocky."

As if to emphasize the point Harrison also daubed the name Rocky on the guitar which he had used – in its original form – on the *Rubber Soul* and *Revolver* albums. With its new design, the guitar made an appearance in the black and white footage from the *All You Need Is Love* television broadcast on June 25, 1967 and then appeared in full colour during the filming – on location at an abandoned RAF station in Kent – of the track 'I Am The Walrus' for the Beatles' *Magical Mystery Tour* broadcast in late 1967.

An Australian company offers to produce exact replicas of Harrison's 'Rocky' using original 1962 Fender guitars and a hand painted reproduction of the Beatles' artwork on to the body – all for around £2,293 while fans can also obtain from America – for just $450 – a piece of custom artwork copying the original Rocky graphics that can be used on an existing guitar.

(Left) George Harrison playing 'Rocky' in Copenhagen on the last night of his tour with Delaney & Bonnie in December 1969.

(Right) The 'coloured guitar' named 'Rocky', featuring George Harrison's dedication to Gene Vincent and Indian mysticism.

John's Afghan jacket

Off on a Magical Mystery Tour

Although the Beatles plan for a television film had been discussed with Brian Epstein, the *Magical Mystery Tour* project was the group's first major venture following the death of their manager and it was at the heart of the first major rift between the 'Fab Four'.

In Epstein's absence, McCartney began to assume leadership of the group and push ahead with an idea for a mystery coach trip around the UK with an oddball set of characters on board and a new selection of songs written and performed by the Beatles. But while Lennon privately expressed his loathing of the whole idea – and the estimated £75,000 cost of what he called "the most expensive home movie ever" – he went along with the project.

"It's about a group of common or garden people on a coach tour around everywhere really and things happen to them." This was Paul's description of the idea that came to him during a trip to America, when he read about *One Flew Over The Cuckoo's Nest* author Ken Kesey's adventures with his 'Merry Pranksters' as they toured the US on a bus.

Travelling without a script but with a film crew, the Beatles invited fan club secretaries and a troupe of actors – including Ivor Cutler, Jessie Robins, Nat Jackley, Maggie Wright plus a party of dwarfs – to join Lennon's son Julian, McCartney's brother Mike McGear and Apple electronics wizard Alexis Mardis on board the bus on September 11, 1967.

During the next four days the bus travelled through Devon and Cornwall, collecting pop star Spencer Davis and his family in Newquay, while the actors worked without any script to produce what McCartney described as "a crazy roly-poly Sixties film."

With the filming completed, including interior sequences shot at West Malling RAF station near Maidstone in Kent, Raymond's Revue Bar in Soho and Nice in the South of France, the Beatles retreated to an editing suite in London where, with the help of film editor Roy Benson, they spent six weeks creating the final product – a 55-minute colour film.

The BBC decided to air it – in black and white – on BBC 2 on Boxing Day 1967, when it was watched by an audience of around 13 million people, plus a number of TV critics who were less than impressed with what they saw. While one commented that he had never seen "such blatant rubbish", another said, "Paul directed, Ringo mugged, John did imitations, George danced a bit and, when the show hit the BBC last week, the audience gagged."

The music they created for the *Magical Mystery Tour* was recorded in Abbey Road throughout September and October, although producer Martin was less than impressed with their efforts. "Some of the sounds weren't very good. Some were brilliant but some were bloody awful." The finished product was a double EP with six tracks – and a special 24-page booklet – which was released in the UK on December 8, sold over 500,000 copies and peaked at number two in the charts.

In America, where the EP was an unknown format, the six original tracks were augmented with five other Beatles songs to create a *Magical Mystery Tour* album, which sold over a million copies and topped the charts for eight weeks. Despite this success, the Beatles film was never shown on US television, following the intense criticism from the British press.

(Right) This Afghan jacket was worn by John Lennon during the filming of the *Magical Mystery Tour* TV special. He later gave it away to American singer Harry Nilsson.

(Overleaf) John Lennon wearing his Afghan jacket at the launch party for the Beatles album *Sgt Pepper's Lonely Hearts Club Band*, held at manager Brian Epstein's London home in May 1967.

Vox Kensington guitar

A one-off used by two Beatles

After importing and distributing European-made guitars throughout the UK since the early 1950s, the British Vox company turned their attention to the idea of making their own guitars. As manufacturers of amplifiers, Vox were well established in the music industry, and by 1961 they had begun producing their first quality electric guitars using the brand names Escort and Consort.

The coffin-shaped Vox Phantom arrived soon after and as most of the emerging British bands – including the Beatles, Rolling Stones, Animals and Dave Clark Five – were regular users of Vox amps, the company had an almost ready-made audience for their new guitars.

Although the Beatles did not turn to Vox's range of guitars, the group did continue to use their amps and wah, wah pedals, while John Lennon had a special Python guitar strap made by the company using black leather and an armoured metal plate. Made in 1964, the Python strap cost around £6.

In 1967 the Beatles set out on their *Magical Mystery Tour* and for the first time they featured a Vox guitar in their collection of instruments. The one-off Kensington guitar was hand built in the Vox factory and displayed at the 1966 British music trade fair before being returned to the factory, where it was customised before being handed over to the Beatles. Vox designer Dick Denney utilized an unusual scroll shape he had seen on an old piano for the mahogany brown body, which came with no identification other than the maker's name.

When journalists gathered at West Malling Air Force base in Kent between September 18 and 24 to report on the band's filming of the track 'I Am The Walrus', they spotted George Harrison playing the Vox prototype Kensington guitar for the first time, although in the final edited version he turned to his Fender Stratocaster.

Two months later – on November 10 – John Lennon was pictured using the same Vox Kensington guitar prototype during a take of the video for the song 'Hello Goodbye', which was shot at the Saville Theatre. However, he used his newly acquired Martin D-28 acoustic guitar in the final version.

Despite making only two appearances with the Beatles, – before being given to Apple electronics expert Alexis "Magic Alex" Mardas – the Kensington guitar was sold at auction in New York in May 2013, where it exceeded its estimated value and fetched US$408,000 (£269,000).

(Right) The unique prototype Vox guitar, which was played by both John Lennon and George Harrison in 1967.

Apple Corps watch

Beatles become business men

When the Beatles returned from their stay with the Maharishi, John Lennon commented "... we had a nice holiday in India and came back rested to play business men." And the business he was talking about – despite once proclaiming, "We'd never start our own label, it's too much trouble – was the company they had created in late 1967.

The Beatles were not the first best-selling pop act to set up their own record or publishing business, but their extraordinary efforts with Apple Corps went a stage further than the record labels set up in the sixties by stars such as Frank Sinatra (Reprise), Sam Cooke (SAR) and Ray Charles (Tangerine).

They launched the forerunner to Apple – under the banner Beatles & Co. – in May 1967 and in November of that year they switched to the name Apple Music Ltd before, in January 1968, finally fixing on Apple Corps Ltd. The company, which was initially located in Wigmore Street in London's West End, was enthusiastically pushed along by McCartney in opposition to the views of both the group's manager Epstein and his song-writing partner Lennon.

Even though both thought the Beatles should focus on music and not on business, Apple Corps came into being four months after Epstein's death. It involved the four band members plus artist manager Robert Stigwood and music agent Vic Lewis, who were both directors of Epstein's NEMS company at the time of his death.

The name Apple was chosen after the simple child's phrase 'A is for Apple' and, as it came at the start of the alphabet, it supposedly represented a new beginning for the Beatles while Paul would say, "It's a pun – apple core – see?" As a logo the Beatles adopted a Granny Smith apple which, as a whole fruit or one cut in half, continues to represent their business dealings to this day.

The company was created as a vehicle through which the Beatles could offset some of their tax liabilities, which at the time were said to be around £3 million. The plan was to invest in businesses that were linked to their own creative activities, and consequently they set up music publishing, record, film and fashion operations.

The famous Apple boutique opened in London's Baker Street in December 1967 and closed seven months later with a massive £10,000 giveaway sale, while Apple Music signed music publishing deals with singer/songwriter Jackie Lomax, the bands Grapefruit and Badfinger and George Harrison.

But thanks to a series of mad-cap ideas – inventor Mad Alex created the Zapple electronics branch – and bizarre management, the company, which moved to offices costing £500,000 at 3 Savile Row in July 1968, began to struggle and put a drain on the band's resources. Lennon once admitted, "I think it's a bit messy and it wants tightening up ... we can't let Apple go on like this", while his fellow band member McCartney later confirmed, "That's why Apple went wrong, because we didn't have the business sense."

However, despite the chaos surrounding Apple throughout the seventies, the Apple Records company provided some financial return with artists such as Mary Hopkin, James Taylor, Billy Preston, Hot Chocolate and Badfinger all signing and recording for the label which employed Peter Asher, half of the pop duo Peter and Gordon and brother of actress (and McCartney's girl-friend) Jane Asher, as head of A&R.

While various solo Beatles' projects were released on the Apple label, the world's most famous and successful group remained signed to EMI. However, they were allowed to use their own company logo on subsequent discs.

(Right) This watch was one of the promotional items produced by Apple Corps, the company started by the Beatles in 1967.

Paul's recording notes for 'Hey Jude'

From Jools to Jude

The Beatles returned the top of the US charts in September 1968 – nine months after their previous chart topper – with 'Hey Jude', which racked up sales of over 4.7 million copies worldwide in just two months.

It was written in the main by McCartney who had Lennon's son Julian in mind when he composed the song after the split between John and Cynthia Lennon. "I thought as a friend of the family I would motor out to Weybridge and tell them that everything was alright", said McCartney. "I had about an hour's drive. I would always turn the radio off and try to make up songs, just in case."

Talking to *Rolling Stone* magazine, McCartney explained how the song had come to him as he was driving. "I started singing 'Hey Jools – don't make it bad'. It was optimistic, a hopeful message for Julian."

Admitting that he eventually changed Jools to Jude – "I just thought a better name was Jude" – McCartney broke down in four sections how he thought the song should be structured. He also identified the instruments and voices for when the Beatles came to record the song over four days in July and August 1968 in both Abbey Road and Trident Studios.

Released in both the UK and US on August 26, 1968, the record was a double first – the first record issued with the group's new Apple logo on the label and the Beatles' longest ever single at seven minutes and 11 seconds. Producer Martin was among the people who believed that singles could not run for that long but when he made his views known he was "shouted down by the boys" with Lennon asking "why not?". The Beatles' producer added, "I couldn't think of an answer really – except the pathetic one that disc jockeys wouldn't play it. He [John] said, 'They will if it's us'."

The single hit the US chart at an all-time high of number 10 and went on to hold the number one spot for nine weeks while in Britain it was the biggest selling record of 1968 and also the group's 15th number one. It remains the Beatles' second most successful single ever with sales of over 10 million – just behind 'I Want To Hold Your Hand' with 12 million.

As Julian Lennon was only five when his parents split and when McCartney wrote 'Hey Jude', it's perhaps not surprising to hear his mother explain, "Funnily enough Julian didn't know about it for years and years and years and then when he realized that 'Hey Jude' was about him, he felt really humbled."

Looking back at the record that almost bears his name, Julian added, "One of dad's closest friends at that time and a confidante and a writing partner was Paul. And he was watching from the wings and decided to write a song about me, or for me, dealing with that particular scenario of the break up and how I must remain, you know, strong and together. It has been an absolute honour to have someone, not only write a song about you, but especially Paul and especially in that circumstance."

(Right) Paul McCartney's notes on the construction of 'Hey Jude' (or Jude as he called it) in four sections, complete with voice and instruments.

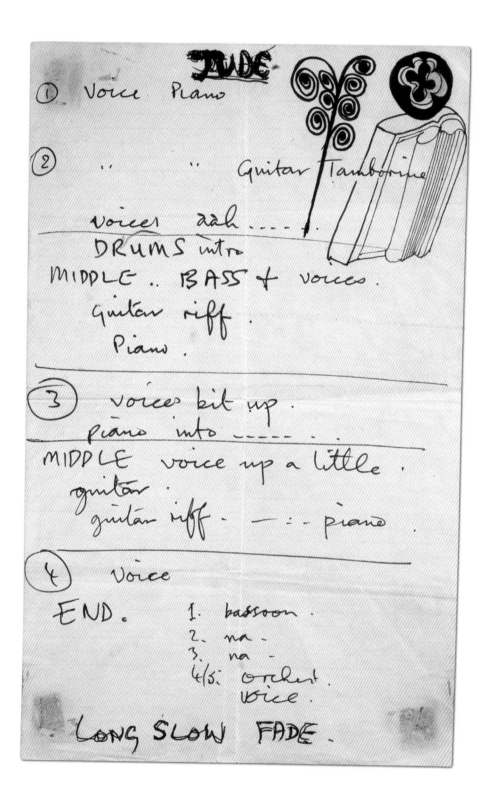

FADE

① Voice Piano

② ‟ ‟ Guitar Tambourine

Voices aah.....
DRUMS intro
MIDDLE .. BASS + voices.
Guitar riff .
Piano .

③ voices bit up .
piano into ----- ..
MIDDLE voice up a little .
guitar .
guitar riff . — :- piano .

④ voice
END . 1. bassoon.
2. na -
3. na -
4/5. orchest.
voice.

LONG SLOW FADE .

The Authorized Biography

"How it all came to pass"

Hunter Davies was working at *The Times* newspaper in September 1966 when he met and interviewed Paul McCartney for his 'Atticus' column. As the author of a book entitled *Here We Go Round The Mulberry Bush*, which was being made into a film, he subsequently approached McCartney about possibly writing some music for the movie's soundtrack.

When McCartney said no, Davies took a chance and asked if he could write a book about the Beatles. This led to him meeting with Epstein, who was agreeable so long as the individual members of the group were happy. With the Beatles and their manager onboard, a contract was agreed that gave the group a third of the book deal which Davies had negotiated with Heinemann.

During 18 months from early 1967 through to 1968, Davies travelled with the Beatles and interviewed friends and family in order to create the first and only authorized biography of the Beatles – a book which in 1968, he later explained, "tried its jumpy, jagged best to describe how it all came to pass."

As the Beatles – and their immediate family – had editorial control and could request cuts in the copy, Davies, after complaints from Lennon's Aunt Mimi about the text covering his childhood and Harrison over the coverage of his religious beliefs, was forced to amend and reduce his copy.

However, finally on September 14, 1968, Davies' finished work was published with a dedication to the Beatles' manager Brian Epstein, who had died in 1967. It was an instant best-seller and it remains in print to this day, following reprints in 1969, 1978, 1979, 1981 and 1985. In the 1981 edition Davies wrote, "I always felt, and still do, that the Beatles as blokes were ordinary blokes put into an extraordinary situation."

Reflecting in 1980 on his time spent with the Beatles in the production of the book, Davies, who also wrote Epstein's obituary for *The Times*, confirmed that the group willingly gave up their time to him although "having to think about their Beatlemania days bored them stiff."

Having moved on to write *The Glory Game* about Tottenham Hotspur football club, a biography of William Wordsworth and, much later on, the official biography of Wayne Rooney, Davies ended his introduction to the 1981 edition of his book by explaining that he resisted the idea of a second Beatles volume. "Their end as Beatles turned out to be far from glorious. It was their rise that mattered. This is the story of their rise."

(Right) Author Hunter Davies spent over 18 months with the Beatles researching material for his original 1968 authorized biography of the group.

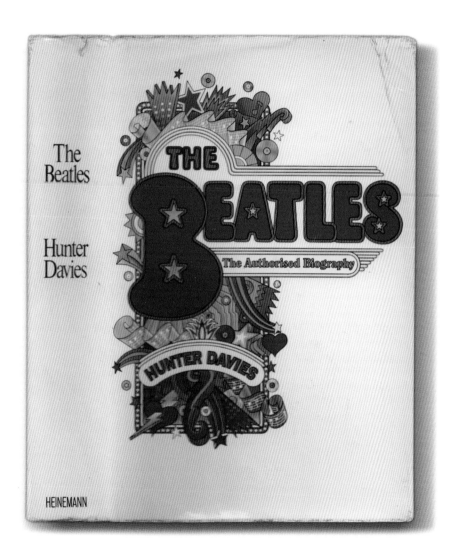

Gered Mankowitz unpublished image
Closing the door on Apple

When the Beatles were looking for a way to end their documentary *Let It Be*, they settled on the idea of one final live performance for the cameras.

"We went on the roof in order to resolve the live concert idea because it was much simpler than going anywhere else," said Harrison while McCartney explained, "So it was suggested that we go up on the roof and do a concert there; then we could all go home."

The event took place on top of the offices of Apple at 3, Savile Row lunch time on Thursday, January 30, 1969. Instruments, recording equipment and film cameras were all collected together with assorted technicians and engineers, some borrowed from Abbey Road, in order that the Beatles, plus keyboard player Billy Preston, could perform and record versions of 'Get Back', 'I've Got a Feeling' and 'Don't Let Me Down' plus 'The One After 909', 'Dig A Pony' and a short excerpt from 'God Save the Queen', during a performance lasting 42 minutes.

One of the engineers on the roof, alongside Glyn Johns, was EMI staff member Alan Parsons, who recalled the event as "one of the greatest and most exciting days of my life – to see the Beatles playing together." While there was no real audience on the roof, just a few friends and family – "we were playing to virtually nothing – to the sky, which was quite nice", recalled McCartney – the crowds gathered down on the pavements in Savile Row as the most famous group in the world played high above them.

Angry businessmen moaned about the noise and one complained to the police who confirmed, "We had so many complaints we sent someone round. A tremendous din was being made." The Beatles were made aware of the police's interest in their show but were determined to keep going. "Good end to the film", reasoned McCartney. "Great! That's an end: 'Beatles Busted On Rooftop Gig'."

Hoping for a dramatic finish to the show, the Beatles had to settle for the police bringing it all to an abrupt close – "I think they pulled the plug and that was the end of the film," said McCartney – but not before Lennon managed to get in a few words: "I'd like to say thanks on behalf of the group and ourselves and I hope we passed the audition."

None of the recordings ever made it on to an official Beatles release other than as part of the *Let It Be* film, although part of one version of 'Get Back' is linked to a studio recording of the song and included on the *Let It Be* album. The version of 'Get Back', that came out as a single on April 11, 1969, was taken from sessions done in the basement studio in Savile Row on the two days before the concert on the roof. While the record contained no producer's credit for either Martin or Johns, who were at both the sessions, it was credited to the Beatles with Billy Preston – the first and only time the name of another artist ever appeared on a Beatles record label.

(Above) The Beatles giving their final performance on the roof of their Savile Row offices in January, 1969.

(Right) Photographer Gerard Mankowitz's picture of the derelict front door to the Apple offices in Savile Row, taken in 1972.

NO VISITORS ALLOWED
IN THIS BUILDING FROM
GROUND FLOOR UPWARDS
WITHOUT THE CONSENT OF
THE GENERAL FOREMAN.
F.W.BARNARD LTD.

Letter to Eastman and Eastman

The beginning of the end

"**K**lein and Apple were bound to meet sooner or later" was how John Lennon saw the situation regarding the American music manager and publisher and the Beatles business empire.

Since the death of Epstein, the Beatles had veered away from appointing another manager but were on the look out for someone to oversee Apple and deal with their recording contracts. Allen Klein had been retained in the 1960s by British acts such as the Dave Clark Five and Herman's Hermits, but it was dealings on behalf of the Rolling Stones – when he negotiated a $1 million advance and a 25% royalty rate (the Beatles were on 15% in the UK and 17.5% in the US) – that had the biggest impact on the Beatles.

"We were impressed by the way he handled the business deals for the Rolling Stones", said Lennon, who led the way by having the first meetings with Klein who had read an article in a music paper when Lennon said, "Apple's losing money every week – if it carries on like this, all of us will be broke in six months." He reacted by getting Lennon's phone number and calling him to set up a meeting in London in January 1969.

Klein had started in the music business in the late 1950s representing the likes of Bobby Darin, Sam Cooke and the Shirelles and eventually setting up his own New York-based ABKCO Industries (short for Allen and Betty Klein), through which he acquired song copyrights and handled the affairs of various artists.

While Lennon was persuaded that Klein should look after the Beatles' affairs – and even sent a note to the chairman of EMI Sir Joseph Lockwood which said, "Dear Joe – from now on Allen Klein handles all my stuff", McCartney favoured his own father-in-law Lee Eastman and in February 1969 the company of Eastman & Eastman was appointed as the Beatles' lawyers.

Slowly Harrison and Starr were persuaded to join forces with Lennon and on April 18, 1969, a letter was sent to Lee Eastman in New York which told him that he was no longer "authorised to represent the Beatles", although he could act for Paul McCartney "personally". The letter then asked for all documents relating to the Beatles to be sent to Klein's ABKCO offices and it was signed by Lennon, Harrison and Starr.

McCartney's reaction to the situation – "I'd fallen out with the others at once over the Klein thing" – was to continue rejecting the American as the manager of the Beatles. "I didn't want him representing me in any way. So it was three against one."

McCartney's objections to Klein were strengthened when he decided to bring in Phil Spector to produce the group's *Let It Be* album and, without consulting the composer, the man behind the legendary 'wall of sound' production technique set about altering 'The Long And Winding Road'.

In fact McCartney was so incensed with the changes Spector made to his song that he wrote to Klein telling him, "In future no one will be allowed to add or subtract from a recording of one of my songs without my permission", and added the sign-off warning, "Don't ever do it again."

Even though Lennon, Harrison and Starr gradually became disenchanted with Klein, it took them a further six years, until 1977, to finally settle all the outstanding litigation and then Starr was moved to admit, "In the end we did get rid of Allen Klein. It cost us a small fortune – but it's one of those things that we found all through life; two people sign a contract and I know exactly what it means and you know exactly what it means but when we come to split up, magically it means something else entirely to one of you."

(Right) The April, 1969 letter signed and sent by John Lennon, Richard Starkey and George Harrison informing Paul McCartney's lawyer (and father-in-law) that he no longer represented the Beatles.

Eastman and Eastman
39 West 54th Street
New York
New York 10019   18th April 1969

<u>Attention Lee Eastman, Esq.</u>

Dear Mr. Eastman,

      This is to inform you of the fact that you are not
authorized to act or to hold yourself out as the attourney
or legal representative of "The Beatles" or of any of the
companies which the Beatles own or control.

      We recognize that you are authorized to act for
Paul McCartney, personally, and in this regard we will
instruct our representatives to give you the fullest co-
operation.

      We would appreciate your forwarding to

            ABKCO Industries Inc.
            1700 Broadway
            New York
            N.Y.

all documents, correspondence and files which you hold
in your possession relating to the affairs of the Beatles,
or any of the companies which the Beatles own or control.

                  Very truly yours,

                  John Lennon

                  Richard Starkey

                  George Harrison

'The Ballad of John and Yoko' gold disc

Two Beatles make a final number one

Released in May 1969, 'The Ballad of John and Yoko' has the distinction of being the first single by the Beatles to be issued in stereo in both the UK and Europe – and the first record never to be mixed for mono.

It was written by Lennon as an autobiographical account of life with Yoko Ono in the early months of 1969 when they got married in Gibraltar and travelled on to France and the Netherlands. "It's something I wrote and it's like an old time ballad. It's just the story of us getting married, going to Paris, going to Amsterdam and it went out as a Beatles track," said Lennon.

In fact, while it was issued as a Beatles single, it was recorded with only Lennon and McCartney in the studio. As Starr was on location filming and Harrison was out of the country, the remaining two members of the group gathered in Abbey Road's studio three on the afternoon of Monday April 14 to record the song that was originally titled 'The Ballad Of John And Yoko (They're Gonna Crucify Me)' in a total of 11 takes.

Lennon did the lead vocal and guitar parts while McCartney played drums, piano, maracas and bass guitar on sessions, which engineer Geoff Emerick recalls as being "very fast" and enhanced by "Paul's great drumming and the speed in which they did it all."

While Lennon explained, "I don't regard it as a separate record scene … it's the Beatles' next single, simple as that. It doesn't mean anything, it just so happened that there were only two of us there".

Neither Harrison or Starr seemed particularly disappointed at not being on the Beatles' twenty-first and first stereo single. "We had no problems with that", said Starr, while Harrison added, "I didn't mind not being invited to the wedding and I didn't mind not being on the record because it was none of my business. If it had been the Ballad of John, George and Yoko, then I would have been on it."

Recorded and mixed in stereo on the same day, the single was released just over six weeks later on May 30 – as a hasty follow up to 'Get Back' – and received a hostile reaction when people heard the line "Christ you know it ain't easy". It was banned by radio stations in Australia and America because of the word 'Christ' although the Spanish Government were unhappy with a reference to Gibraltar as being 'near Spain' rather than part of the country as they claim

Despite the concern over the lyrics, 'The Ballad of John and Yoko' still reached number eight in America while in the UK it was set to become the Beatles 17th and last ever number one hit single.

(Right) An American gold disc for one million sales of 'The Ballad of John and Yoko', which was the Beatles' first stereo single and their last UK number one.

John's Honda Monkey motorbike
Tittenhurst Park remembered

Back in 1967 Ringo Starr had rented his London flat to John Lennon and Yoko Ono, and six years later the group's rhythm guitarist and singer returned the favour by selling his house to the band's drummer.

Tittenhurst Park was a Georgian manor house built on a 72-acre site in Sunninghill near Ascot and Lennon bought it after selling Kenwood, the house he shared with Cynthia and Julian Lennon, and spending some time in Starr's flat at Montagu Square. He paid £145,000 for the property and spent more than that renovating the house and grounds and installing his own recording studio.

On August 22, 1969 – just over a week after the Lennons moved in – the Beatles gathered at Tittenhurst for what turned out to an historic photo session – it was to be the last time the four of them were photographed together. "It was just a photo session", said Ringo. "I wasn't there thinking 'OK this is the last photo session'", while McCartney recalled, "Linda shot some 16mm footage on my camera that turned out to be the last film taken."

Some of the shots taken inside and outside the house and around the gardens of Tittenhurst Park by American photographer Ethan Russell and veteran Fleet Street snapper Monte Fresco were used on the front and back covers of the compilation album *Hey Jude*, which was issued in 1970 by Capitol Records in the US only, where it peaked at number two behind Simon & Garfunkel's *Bridge Over Troubled Water*.

Just over a week after the photo shoot, Bob Dylan visited the Lennons in their Berkshire home after his August 31 performance at the 1969 Isle of Wight festival. It was to be the last time the two performers got together and Lennon seemingly had an idea to involve him in a session. "He came over to our house with George (Harrison) after the Isle of Wight and when I had written 'Cold Turkey'. I was trying to get him to record. We had just put him on piano for 'Cold Turkey' to make a rough tape, but his wife was pregnant or something and they left."

The film to promote Lennon's 1971 solo song 'Imagine', was also shot inside Tittenhurst Park, where John used to take his son Julian for rides on his Honda Monkey motorbike. Lennon also adopted Tittenhurst Park as the business address of his Bag Productions company and installed his Ascot Sound Studio. However, as he decided to spend more time in America, Lennon eventually decided to get rid of the house, and in 1973 Starr bought the property from his band mate and lived there with his first wife Maureen Cox until their divorce in 1975.

Bag Productions Inc.
Tittenhurst Park,
Ascot, Berkshire.
Ascot 23022

(Above) A business card for John Lennon's Bag Productions company, which he based at Tittenhurst Park.

(Right) The Honda Monkey bike that John Lennon drove around Tittenhurst Park, with his son Julian as a passenger.

John's acoustic guitar

Drawing on his Gibson

George Harrison wasn't the only member of the Beatles who decided on a paint job for his guitar in advance of the global TV broadcast of *All You Need Is Love* in 1967. Lennon took one of his favourite Gibson J-160E guitars and called upon the group's preferred design team the Fool to hand paint a new design on the guitar, following his own experimental effort to spray paint a greyish-white finish on the back of his earlier Epiphone Casino guitar.

The Fool – a design partnership featuring Dutch artists Marike Koger and Josje Leeger plus Canadian Barry Finch and Simon Hayes – worked on cars, clothes and houses owned by the group members and their partners. They had been commissioned by Brian Epstein to work on the Saville Theatre, which he took over in April 1965 and also created the outfits worn by the Beatles during the *All You Need Is Love* show.

Their work on Lennon's guitar – symmetrical waves in two shades of blue separated by red lines – was first seen during *All You Need Is Love*. The instrument, however, stayed on the studio floor and was never played during the broadcast because, it's claimed, Lennon was too nervous to sing live and play the guitar at the same time.

In 1968 Lennon had another go at do-it-yourself guitar painting when he stripped the same Gibson J-160E back to its natural wood finish and then drew caricatures of himself and Yoko Ono on the body of the guitar and also autographed his handiwork. The guitar was seen by the public during the couple's second bed-in at the Hotel Reine-Elizabeth in Montreal which began in late May and ran through to early June in 1969.

The newly married Lennon and Ono had held their first bed-in during their honeymoon in March 1969 when they spent five days – between March 25 and 31 – in bed in the Presidential Suite of the Amsterdam Hilton hotel to promote world peace to the world's media, who were invited to the room from 9am until 9pm every day.

During the follow-up bed-in – held over seven days in four rooms of the Canadian hotel – Lennon used his newly illustrated Gibson guitar on the recording of 'Give Peace A Chance' which was made on a portable four-track machine with the help of guests such as culture guru Timothy Leary, British singer Petula Clark, writer Allen Ginsberg and comedian Dick Gregory.

The finished version of 'Give Peace A Chance', released under the banner of Lennon's new group the Plastic Ono Band, was still credited as a Lennon/McCartney composition despite it being written by Lennon with some contributions from Ono. "I was guilty enough to give to McCartney credit as co-writer on my first independent single instead of giving it to Yoko who had actually co-authored it," explained Lennon.

The single was issued on July 4, 1969 and peaked at number two in the UK, also reaching the US top twenty.

(Above) The newly-married John Lennon and Yoko Ono hold their first bed-in at the Amsterdam Hilton hotel in March 1969.

(Right) The Gibson J-160E acoustic guitar which John Lennon adorned with caricatures of himself and Yoko.

Microphone from Abbey Road

George has the final word

After more than seven years of regular recording sessions at Abbey Road Studios, the Beatles got together in their favourite north London hang-out for the final time on August 20, 1969.

They were there on that Wednesday afternoon to oversee the final mixing of a song that they began working on in Trident Studios in February, but completed in the studio-three control room with producer George Martin, engineers Geoff Emerick and Phil McDonald and second engineer Alan Parsons in attendance.

As it wasn't an actual recording session – 'I Want You (She's So Heavy)' had been almost finished in April and was finally completed on August 11, using the tapes recorded in February – Lennon, McCartney, Harrison and Starr gathered in the studio one last time to finalize the stereo mixing of the track and to assemble the songs and running order for their last ever album.

The recording of 'I Want You', a song written by Lennon but as ever credited to Lennon/McCartney, involved more than 35 takes done at Trident plus subsequent overdubbing, including Billy Preston's keyboards and Lennon's Moog synthesizer sound effects to create the final version, which lasted over eight minutes. "We used the moog synthesizer on the end of 'I Want You'. That machine can do all sounds and all ranges of sounds. It's like a robot," said Lennon.

Although the last time all four Beatles were together in Abbey Road was in the smaller studio three, it had been in the larger studio two where they had spent most of the time during their years of recording at EMI's north London studio complex. It was in this studio where they assembled on August 8, 1969 to record tracks for the album *Abbey Road* but only after they had spent the part of the morning out in the street being photographed for the album's famous cover shot.

In January 1970, the final Beatles recording session took place in studio two, completing Harrison's song 'I Me Mine'.

(Above) One of the Neumann microphones used by the Beatles during their sessions in the Abbey Road studios.

(Right) George Harrison sang the vocals on his song 'I Me Mine' – the last track recorded by the Beatles in Abbey Road.

Invite to Bag One

Getting into the arts

It was John Dunbar, the former husband of singer Marianne Faithfull, who got John Lennon involved in London's swingin' sixties avant-garde art scene when, in November 1966, he invited him to an exhibition entitled 'Unfinished Paintings & Objects by Yoko Ono'. As he wandered around the gallery on the night before the exhibition opened, Lennon, by his own admission, "wasn't quite sure what it was about".

Later Dunbar introduced him to the Japanese artist Yoko Ono, who involved the Beatle with some of her exhibits, including one called 'Hammer A Nail In'. When Lennon asked if he could hammer in a nail, Yoko Ono replied that he could if he paid her five shillings. Lennon's response was to offer her an imaginary five shillings in exchange for being allowed to hammer in an imaginary nail. "And that's when we really met", said Lennon. "That's when we locked eyes and she got it and I got it and that was it."

Speaking later Ono, who by her own admission had little interest in pop music – "the Beatles thing, rock 'n' roll, had passed me by" – recalled her first meeting with Lennon. "He played exactly the same mind game as me." Lennon maintained his interest in Ono's art by sponsoring her 'Half-Wind Show' and he then organized the nude photograph of the two of them that appeared as the cover of the album *Two Virgins*.

In January 1970 an exhibition of 14 erotic lithographs by Lennon opened at the London Art Gallery in New Bond Street but on January 16 – the day after it opened – detectives from Scotland Yard raided the gallery and confiscated eight of the lithographs.

While the six remaining lithographs remained on show until the scheduled end of the gallery run on January 25. All 14 were put on display in Detroit with incident: the London Art Gallery was charged with showing "an indecent exhibition". Finally in April 1970 the case was dismissed in favour of the London Art Gallery and all the lithographs were returned to Lennon. At the time sets of the lithographs sold for over £500 and in 2008 a catalogue from the exhibition in London, signed by Lennon, sold for £25,000.

Dunbar was also involved with writer Barry Miles and Peter Asher, a singer who was the brother of Paul McCartney's girlfriend Jane Asher, and between them they opened the Indica Gallery and Bookshop in September 1965 in Mason's Yard in the fashionable St James area of London, close to the popular pop stars hang-out of the Scotch of St James' Club.

From the earliest days McCartney – the only Beatle to remain in central London – was a supporter of the venture, even designing the shop's wrapping paper and helping to put up shelves and plaster walls. "I stayed in London and got into the arts scene and papers like the *International Times*," recalled McCartney. According to Miles, he also spent hours in the shop. "He would come in late at night from a gig and browse among the books and just leave a note saying what he had taken."

The *International Times* (IT) newspaper was launched – with Miles as an editor and McCartney as a financial backer who was credited in the staff box under the name 'Ian Iachimoe' – with an all-night rave at Chalk Farm Roundhouse on October 15, 1966.

When the paper began to run into financial difficulties, it was McCartney who came up with a rescue plan. He said to Miles, "If you interview me then you'll be able to get advertising from record companies" and this was followed by a second interview with George Harrison. Eventually the *International Times*, following complaints from *The Times* newspaper, changed its name to just *IT*.

(Right) An invitation to the exhibition of John Lennon's lithography at the London Arts Gallery, which was raided and shut down by the police in 1970.

JOHN & YOKO ONO LENNON
and The Directors of London Arts Gallery
invite you to the
world premier exhibition of

Bag One

Fourteen original signed lithographs

January 15 – January 28

The London Arts Gallery
22 New Bond Street, London W.1.
A MEMBER OF THE LONDON ARTS GROUP

Get Back LP

What *Let It Be* could have been

The strange out of order finale to the Beatles career – releasing the last two albums they recorded in reverse order – came about as a result of their enthusiasm to create a television documentary and a live recording under the banner 'Get Back'.

But internal squabbles – including George Harrison walking out on the group – and differences of opinion marred the project to the extent that *Get Back* was finally abandoned after a year's work in early January 1970, when a master tape of the final 15 songs had been compiled ready for release.

But all was not lost as the Beatles rescued most of the songs from the sessions done in the Apple, Olympic and Abbey Road studios – under the direction of producer George Martin and engineer Glyn Johns – and transferred to them to their new *Let It Be* album project which was preceded by the release of the title track as a single.

The song was finally completed on January 4, 1970 which goes down in history as the day when the Beatles actually recorded together for the last time as a band albeit without Lennon who was on holiday. The other three assembled between 2.30pm and 4pm in, appropriately, Abbey Road's studio two, the place where it all started for them back in June 1962.

Working with a basic track that was over a year old, they added brass, guitars, vocals and cellos to complete the record which would turn out to be the last single released in Britain during the group's time together. It swept to number two in the UK charts and brought to an end a run of 23 successive top-five hit singles including 17 number ones.

Two weeks after their final UK single release, the Beatles resumed work on the album *Let It Be* when they took 12 songs from *Get Back* and handed them over to the notoriously temperamental American producer Phil Spector to record, re-record and remix for the re-named

project. The man who invented the 'wall of sound' was something of a surprise choice to succeed Martin, but Lennon in particular was a huge fan of Spector's work even though he commented, "The least you could call him is eccentric and that's coming from somebody who's barmy."

Between March 23 and April 2, 1970 Spector worked on the various Beatles tracks and his finished work was recognized by Starr who said, "I like what Phil did actually. There's no point in bringing him in if you're not going to like the way he does it" while Lennon stated, "... he was given the shittiest load of badly recorded shit with a lousy feeling to it ever and he made a something out of it."

Less impressed was Martin who remarked, "I didn't like Phil Spector's *Let It Be* at all. It was bringing the Beatles records down a peg – that's what I thought", while McCartney observed, "I heard the Spector version again recently and it sounded terrible." Equally unimpressed was NME whose reviewer described the album as "a cardboard tombstone" and a "sad and tatty end to a musical fusion".

The last Beatles album was finally released on May 8, 1970, with US advance orders totalling over $3.7 million. It was number one in America for four weeks and brought to an end an incredible run of 19 top three albums in America in just over six years. It also topped the British chart for three weeks, bringing the Beatles their 11th UK top three album between 1963 and 1970.

(Right) The unreleased Beatles *Get Back* album – essentially an up-dated version of their first album cover – which was eventually abandoned in favour of *Let It Be*.

The *Daily Mirror*, April 10, 1970

Paul quits the Beatles

The first hint that all was not well with the Beatles came in August 1968, when Ringo Starr quit during the recording of the so-called *White Album*. He returned within a few days but then George Harrison left briefly in 1969 during the making of *Let It Be*. There followed the arrival of Allen Klein and the dispute between Paul McCartney and his three bandmates over who was going to manage the Beatles, which also raised the question: would there be any more Beatles to manage?

Things were brought to a head on April 9, 1970, when McCartney issued his first solo album, *McCartney*, almost simultaneously with the group's final *Let It Be* album and, in a prepared printed interview which accompanied the album, said he had no plans for either a new single or album with the Beatles, did not foresee a time when he would work with John Lennon again and, in answer to the question 'Is your break with the Beatles temporary or permanent, due to personal differences or musical ones?', he said, "Personal differences, business differences, musical differences – but most of all because I have a better time with my family. Temporary or permanent? I really don't know."

The reaction in the next day's papers were headlines saying "Paul is Quitting the Beatles" and "The Beatles Are Breaking Up" while McCartney was quickly blamed as the man 'who broke up the Beatles'. In fact the breakdown in relations following Lennon, Harrison and Starr appointing Klein as their business manager and McCartney retaining his father-in-law John Eastman pointed to only one solution – to finally dissolve the business partnership that was the Beatles.

Four months later – in August 1970 – McCartney sent a letter to *Melody Maker* which made his position clear. "In order to put out of its misery the limping dog of a news story which has been dragging itself across your pages for the past year, my answer to the question 'will the Beatles get together again?' is 'No'."

Finally, on the last day of December 1970, McCartney filed a suit in the Chancery Division of the High Court of Justice against the rest of the group to dissolve the Beatles & Co partnership, which had been established in 1967, and have a receiver appointed to handle the group's affairs.

The case – number 1970 No.6315 – opened on January 19, 1971 and was adjourned on the same day for a month during which time, according to Judge Mr Justice Stamp, the royalty income of the Beatles would remain frozen. The hearing resumed in February and after nearly two weeks of evidence, the judge brought proceedings to an end and reserved his judgement, returning on March 12, 1971 to give his final ruling.

Mr Justice Stamp concluded that Lennon, Harrison and Starr had appointed Klein without consulting McCartney. He also decided that the three Beatles agreeing to Klein taking more commission than was previously agreed was a "grave breach" of their responsibilities to McCartney.

In May 1971 Lennon, Harrison and Starr abandoned their plans to launch an appeal against McCartney's action to dissolve the partnership and at the one-day hearing they were ordered to pay their ex-partner's costs while Lord Justice Russell said he hoped that all four Beatles would reach a sensible agreement before adding, "My only disappointment is that I am not able to joke about preserving the Status Quo – which is the name of another pop group."

With that one-liner the Beatles were effectively no more and, although they went their separate solo ways, it would not be until 1975 that the Beatles & Co partnership was formally dissolved in a private High Court hearing.

(Right) Paul McCartney made the headlines when he released his first solo album in 1970 and announced that he had no plans to make any more records with the Beatles.

DAILY Mirror

5d. Friday, April 10, 1970 ✦ ✦ ✦ No. 20,616

Kidnappers send girl home by taxi

PAUL QUITS THE BEATLES

McCartney . . . a deadlock over policy with John Lennon

By DON SHORT

PAUL McCARTNEY has quit the Beatles. The shock news must mean the end of Britain's most famous pop group, which has been idolised by millions the world over for nearly ten years.

Today 28-year-old McCartney will announce his decision, and the reasons for it, in a no-holds-barred statement.

It follows months of strife over policy in Apple, the Beatles' controlling organisation, and an ever-growing rift between McCartney and his songwriting partner, John Lennon.

McCartney and Lennon are rated one of the greatest popular songwriting teams of the century.

But there is little doubt that McCartney's decision will bring it to an end.

Safe

In his statement, which consists of a series of answers to questions, Mcartney says:

"I have no future plans to record or appear with The Beatles again. Or to write any more music with John."

Last night the statement was locked up in a safe at Apple headquarters in Savile-row, Mayfair—in the very rooms where the Beatles' break-up began.

The Beatles decided to appoint a "business adviser." Eventually they settled for American Allen Klein.

His appointment was strongly resisted by Paul, who sought the job for his father-in-law, American attorney Lee Eastman.

After a meeting in London Paul was out-voted 3-1 by John, and the other Beatles, George Harrison and Ringo Starr.

In his statement today Paul will say what he feels

'Deeply cut up' after policy row

about it all and his attitudes towards Mr. Klein.

Since the Klein appointment, Paul has refused to go to the Apple offices to work daily.

He kept silent and stayed at his St. John's Wood home with his photographer wife Linda, her daughter Heather, and their own baby Mary. He was obviously deeply cut up.

Close friends tried to pacify John and Paul. But August last year was the last time they were to work together — when they collaborated on the "Abbey Road" album.

One friend said: "The atmosphere is distinctly cool. They do not hate one another. This is just deadlock over policy."

Geniuses

Dick James, managing director of Northern Songs, publishers of the Lennon-McCartney songs, told me:

"It could mean that in competition with each other they will even write greater songs. They are both geniuses—Paul a melodic one and John in an inventive capacity."

There were other elements

that hastened Paul's decision to quit. John Lennon, on his marriage to Yoko Ono, set out on projects of his own. Ringo went into films, and George stepped in as a record producer.

Today McCartney will reveal his own plans for a solo programme.

It will include a full-length film based on the much-loved children's book character Rupert.

Secret

But the very first project is an album of his own compositions.

It is simply called "McCartney" which he not only wrote, but produced entirely himself.

He played every instrument to be heard on the 14 tracks. His wife Linda added vocal harmonies.

The whole operation has been in secret. When the first 200 copies were pressed this week McCartney collected them all from the factory — so they could not be "poached."

By tomorrow hundreds of thousands will be rushed across the world. The first should reach Britain's shops by Monday morning.

CAROLE BENAINOUS, the little girl pictured with her mother yesterday, was held by kidnappers for more than twenty hours.

But the kidnappers sent six-year-old Carole home by taxi after her wealthy father had left £2,000 ransom money on a lonely road outside Paris.

The drama began on Wednesday when Carole and her mother, Madame Jeanine Benainous, stopped a taxi outside their Paris home to take Carole to school.

The driver was a kidnapper—

and he drove Carole to a secret hideout outside the city.

Four hours later the kidnappers rang Carole's home demanding the money for her release. They rang again twice through the night.

After the third call, Carole's company director father Rene decided to follow the kidnappers' instructions. He told police to keep away, drove to the pre-arranged spot, and left the cash.

A few hours later Carole returned home. She was unharmed, but very tired.

Last night a massive police hunt was going on for the kidnappers.

Postcard from John

An untrue rumour

Around the same time as Paul McCartney began his campaign to break up the Beatles in January 1971, John Lennon wrote a note to the boss of Capitol Records in America urging him to support Yoko Ono's new album and also making clear his feelings on the subject of any sort of Beatles reunion.

Before he took over as head of Capitol, Bhaskar Menon had headed up EMI's company in India, where he met and spent time with the Beatles and – in January 1968 – had travelled from Calcutta (now Kolkata) to Bombay (now Mumbai) with a two-track stereo recording machine for George Harrison to use on his *Wonderwall* soundtrack album. In early 1971 – after the release of the album *Yoko Ono – Plastic Ono Band* – Lennon apparently wrote to Menon, who was based in Los Angeles in the company's famous Capitol Tower headquarters, making it clear that the idea of the Beatles ever getting together again was an "unfounded, untrue rumour".

Even after the Beatles had legally been disbanded in May 1971, the disagreements and arguments between Lennon and his former song-writing partner Paul McCartney continued – albeit in the pages of the best-selling music paper *Melody Maker*. Speaking in November 1971, McCartney said, "I just wanted the four of us to get together somewhere and sign a piece of paper saying 'it's all over' and we want to divide the money four ways." Confirming his plan that "no one else would be there, not even Linda or Yoko or Allen Klein", McCartney added, "We'd just sign the paper and hand it on to the business people and let them sort it out." He then told the journalist, "That's all I want now, but John won't do it."

A month later Lennon wrote a reply – which he sent to *Melody Maker* on the condition that the paper printed it in full – in which he pointed out that breaking up the group and sharing out the money was not as easy as his former bandmate thought. "Maybe there's an answer there somewhere, but for the millionth time in these past few years I repeat, 'What about the TAX?' It's all very well playing the 'simple honest ole Paul' in *Melody Maker*, but you know damn well we can't just sign a bit of paper."

He then explained, "You say 'John won't do it'. I will if you indemnify us against the tax man! Anyway you know that after we have OUR meeting, the fucking lawyers will have to implement whatever we agree on, right?" And in his postscript Lennon made the position clear regarding his wife. "The bit that really puzzled us was asking to meet WITHOUT LINDA AND YOKO. I thought you'd have understood BY NOW that I'm JOHNANDYOKO."

With that, the public correspondence between the two musicians who created most of the music that made the Beatles rich and famous ended. Subsequently, there was no reunion of any kind until McCartney gathered Harrison and Starr in a studio in 1995 to re-work Lennon's 1977 song 'Free As a Bird'.

(Right) John Lennon's postcard to the head of Capitol Records, Bhaskar Menon, the text of which includes his comments on the subject of 'the Beatles getting together again.'

Dear, Bhaskar

How are you? good! Please put 'Capital Power' behind Yoko's great new Pop album (read Melody Maker review – N. Y. Times etc). by the way the 'Beatles getting together again' rumour is rife again – even Capitol man Tom WEBKER (chicago) is CONFIRMING such an unfounded untrue rumour – anyway 'give Yoko a chance' – Happy New Year love John + Yoko

Index

Acknowledgements & Photography credits

Brian Southall would like to thank all those people who extended him a helping hand in the preparation and writing of this book while also acknowledging the assistance and efforts of the White Feather Foundation: www.whitefeatherfoundation.com

Particular thanks must go to Roland Hall at Carlton Books and the team of people whose considerable efforts helped create this book and to Pete Nash for his invaluable assistance. I would also like to say thanks to the British Library and their comprehensive files of back issues of *Melody Maker*, *New Musical Express* and *Record Retailer* alongside the following published works:

Abbey Road by Brian Southall (Patrick Stephens 1982); *The Beatles* by Hunter Davies (Granada 1969); *The Beatles Anthology* by The Beatles (Cassell & Co 2000); *The Beatles Encyclopedia* by Bill Harry (Virgin 1992); *Beatles Gear* by Andy Babiuk (Backbeat Books 2001); *The Beatles Live!* By Mark Lewisohn (Pavilion 1986); *The Beatles Recording Sessions* by Mark Lewisohn (Hamlyn 198); *Billboard Book of Number One Hits* by Fred Bronson (Billboard 1997); *Billboard Book of Number One Albums* by Craig Rosen (Billboard 1996); *Brian Epstein: The Man Who Made The Beatles* by Ray Coleman (Viking 1989); *Paul McCartney Many Years From Now* by Barry Miles (Secker & Warburg 1997); *Northern Songs* by Brian Southall (Omnibus 2007); *Rock Atlas* by David Roberts (Clarksdale 2012).

The publishers would like to thank the following sources for their kind permission to reproduce the pictures in this book.

Alamy: Keystone Pictures USA: 10-11; /Theodore Liasi: 179; /TracksImages.com: 87; /**By kind permission of Bonhams:** 9, 35, 66, 67, 157, 158-159; /**Carlton Books Ltd: Photography by Karl Adamson:** 13 (top right), 13 (bottom), 14, 15, 43, 51, 57, 59, 77, 81, 90, 96, 97, 99 (top), 99 (bottom), 100, 101, 102, 103, 112, 113, 123, 133, 137, 139, 140, 151, 166, 167, 173, 181 (top), 193, 207, 212, 233, 249; /**Corbis:** Buddy Mays: 191; /**Getty Images:** Archive Photos: 25; /Blank Archives: 192; /Peter Bruchmann/K & K Ulf Kruger OHG/Redferns: 36; /Christies: 237; /Cummings Archives: 49-50; /John Downing: 224-225; /Express: 234; /GAB Archive: 29, 144-145; /John Hoppy Hopkins/Redferns: 62-63; /Hulton Archive: 18-19; /Keystone/Hulton Archive: 120-121, 168-169; /K & K Ulf Kruger OHG: 20; /Michael Ochs Archives: 34, 148-149, 160, 181 (centre), 182-183; /Max Nash/AFP: 164; /Terry O'Neill: 40-41, 88-89; /Nigel Osbourne/Redferns: 21, 33, 39, 221, 243; /Jan Persson/Redferns: 220; /Ellen Piel/K & K/ Redferns: 44-45; /David Redfern/Redferns: 32, 93, 141; /TS Productions: 68; /Rowland Scherman: 152-153; /Len Trievnor/Express: 114-115; / Bob Whitaker/Hulton Archive: 196-197; /**Photograph courtesy of Heritage auctions, www.ha.com:** 147; /**Magnum Photos:** © David Hurn: 111-112; /© **Julian Lennon, The White Feather Foundation:** 172, 177, 185, 211, 217, 219, 223, 229, 239, 241; /© **Gered Mankowitz:** 235; /**Massygo:** 86; / **Mirrorpix:** 251; /**The Music Center Archives/Otto Rothschild Collection:** 180; /**Peter Nash:** 13 (top left), 150, 256; /**The National Archives:** 199; /**Press Association Images:** S&G Barratts: 128-129; /Peter Byrne/PA Archive: 26, 27; /Christies/PA Archive: 3, 213; /PA Archive: 165, 171, 203, 208; /**Private Collection:** 85, 95; /**Copyrighted 2013. PROMETHEUS Global Media LLC 98683:413JM:** 155; /**Rex Features:** 72-73, 216, 240; / Peter Brooker: 244; /Bournemouth News: 65 (top), 65 (bottom); /Crollalanza: 242; /Jim Duxbury: 175 (bottom); /ITV: 7, 131; /Julien's Auctions: 109 (left), 109 (right), 162, 163, 205, 227, 253; /David Magnus: 245; /Steve Poole/Daily Mail: 55;Mark Sumner: 16; /Sipa Press: 24; /**Collection Herbert Hauke, www.rockmuseum.de:** 53, 195; /**Ron Jones Associates/Merseyside Photo Library:** © Don Valentine: 78; /**Sotheby's Picture Library:** 23, 215, 231; /**TracksImages.com:** 17 (top & bottom), 30, 31, 37, 47 (top), 47 (bottom), 50, 60 (top), 60 (bottom), 69, 71, 75 (top), 75 (bottom), 79, 83, 91, 92, 104, 105, 106, 107, 117, 118 (left), 118 (right), 119, 127 (top), 127 (bottom), 130, 135 (top), 135 (bottom), 143 (top), 143 (bottom), 161 (left), 161 (right), 175 (top), 181 (bottom), 187, 189 (6 photographs), 200, 201, 206, 209, 247.

Every effort has been made to acknowledge correctly and contact the source and/or copyright holder of each picture and Carlton Books Limited apologises for any unintentional errors or omissions, which will be corrected in future editions of this book.